Hockey Drills FOR Scoring

Newell Brown
Chicago Blackhawks

Vern Stenlund, EdD
Windsor Spitfires
Huron Hockey School

Human Kinetics

Library of Congress Cataloging-in-Publication Data

Brown, Newell, 1962–
    Hockey drills for scoring / Newell Brown, K. Vern Stenlund.
        p.   cm. -- (Hockey drills)
    ISBN 0-88011-736-2
    1. Hockey--Training.   I. Stenlund, K. Vern.   II. Title.
    III. Series: Hockey drills (Champaign, Ill.)
    GV848.3.B76   1997
    796.968'07--dc21   97-13802
                                                                    CIP

ISBN: 0-88011-736-2

Developmental Editor: Kirby Mittelmeier; **Assistant Editor:** Jennifer Stallard; **Editorial Assistant:** Jennifer Hemphill; **Copyeditor:** Allan Gooch; **Proofreader:** Tom Long; **Graphic Designer:** Judy Henderson; **Graphic Artist:** Kathleen Boudreau-Fuoss; **Photo Editor:** Boyd La Foon; **Cover Designer:** Jack Davis; **Photographer (cover):** Tim De Frisco; **Photographer (interior):** Gerry Marentette; **Mac Art Illustrator:** Craig Ronto; **Printer:** United Graphics

Human Kinetics books are available at special discounts for bulk purchase. Special editions or book excerpts can also be created to specification. For details, contact the Special Sales Manager at Human Kinetics.

Printed in the United States of America   10   9   8   7   6   5

Human Kinetics
Web site: www.humankinetics.com

United States: Human Kinetics, P.O. Box 5076, Champaign, IL 61825-5076
800-747-4457
e-mail: humank@hkusa.com

Canada: Human Kinetics, 475 Devonshire Road, Unit 100, Windsor, ON N8Y 2L5
800-465-7301 (in Canada only)
e-mail: orders@hkcanada.com

Europe: Human Kinetics, Units C2/C3 Wira Business Park, West Park Ring Road
Leeds LS16 6EB, United Kingdom
+44 (0) 113 278 1708
e-mail: hk@hkeurope.com

Australia: Human Kinetics, 57A Price Avenue, Lower Mitcham, South Australia 5062
08 8277 1555
e-mail: liahka@senet.com.au

New Zealand: Human Kinetics, P.O. Box 105-231, Auckland Central
09-523-3462
e-mail: hkp@ihug.co.nz

Contents

Drill Finder

The Drill Finder is a reference for quick identification of the different aspects of scoring described in each drill. Although you will find that the drills in this book have been organized within specific chapters that deal with a unique aspect of scoring, in many cases you can use a drill to practice other skill areas or to provide more challenge. Remember to look at the "Drill Progressions" section of the drills for ways to adapt them to your own objectives. By focusing on the peripheral skills included in each drill, you may find it easier to organize efficient practices using a variety of themes.

Drill #	Drill	Half- or full-ice	Mechanics	Angles	Timing	Pressure	Conditioning	Adv. skills	Passing	Fun
1	Hit the Target	H	X							
2	Dead Puck	H	X							
3	Target Board	H	X							
4	The Combo	F	X		X					
5	The Wave	H	X	X	X					
6	Circle Shots	H	X	X	X				X	
7	Two-Line Straight	F	X		X	X			X	
8	Numbers Game	F	X	X	X					X
9	Full-Ice Loop	F	X				X			
10	Center Cuts	H	X	X	X					
11	Full Rapid Fire	F	X	X	X		X			
12	Full-Ice Angles	F	X	X	X		X		X	
13	Team Rockets	F	X	X	X		X			
14	Double Wing	H	X	X	X		X		X	
15	Against the Grain	H		X	X			X	X	
16	Razer's Edge	H		X	X		X	X	X	
17	Razer's Edge II	H		X	X		X	X	X	
18	Newt's Delay	H		X	X		X	X	X	
19	Newt's Double 'D'	H		X	X		X	X	X	
20	Empty Tank	F	X	X	X		X			X
21	Five-Puck Finish	H		X	X		X			X
22	Heads Up	H	X	X	X		X			X
23	Ladder Game	F			X	X	X	X	X	X
24	Survival	F			X	X	X			X
25	Coaches' Choice	F				X	X	X	X	X
26	Wild Card 3-on-3	F		X	X	X			X	X
27	Safe House 3-on-3	H		X	X	X		X	X	X
28	Buzz Saw	H		X	X	X		X	X	X
29	Special Teams Rally	F		X	X	X	X	X	X	X
30	Colorado Specials	F		X	X	X	X	X	X	X
31	Robertson's Roast	H	X			X				
32	Grease	H		X	X	X	X	X	X	
33	Grease Fire	H		X	X	X	X	X	X	
34	Grunt Drill	F	X	X		X	X			
35	Back Draft	F		X	X	X	X	X	X	

Drill #	Drill	Half- or full-ice	Mechanics	Angles	Timing	Pressure	Conditioning	Adv. skills	Passing	Fun
36	The Vise	H	X	X	X	X	X	X		
37	Circle War	F		X	X	X	X			
38	On Fire	F		X	X	X	X	X		
39	Shut Down	F		X	X	X	X	X	X	
40	Beat the Box	H		X	X	X	X	X	X	X
41	Flyer Pepper	H	X	X	X			X		
42	Three-Shot Panic	H		X	X		X	X	X	
43	Jackal 2-on-2	F		X	X	X	X	X	X	
44	Back-Door Quarterback	H		X	X			X	X	X
45	Quiet Zone I	H		X	X			X	X	X
46	Curl Returns	H			X			X	X	
47	Two-Player Dash	F		X			X		X	
48	Trapshooting	H		X	X			X	X	X
49	Assassin	H		X	X			X	X	X
50	Merry-Go-Round	F		X	X		X	X	X	
51	Deke Showdown	H	X	X	X					X
52	Double-End Dekes	F			X	X	X			X
53	Airmail	H	X	X	X				X	X
54	Airmail 2-on-1	F			X	X	X		X	
55	Quiet-Zone Redirect	H		X	X			X	X	X
56	Jam City	H	X	X	X					X
57	Three-Line Redirects & Tips	H	X	X	X					
58	Three-Line Escape	H		X	X			X	X	
59	Three-Line Delay	F		X	X			X		
60	Sator's Transition	F		X	X		X	X	X	X
61	Center Retreats	H		X	X		X	X		
62	The Weave	F			X		X		X	
63	Three-Rush Throttle	F	X		X		X		X	X
64	Bullet Screens	F			X		X		X	X
65	Hit the Hole 2-on-0	F		X	X		X		X	X
66	Walsh's 2-on-1	F		X	X	X	X	X	X	X
67	Backcheck 3-on-2	F		X	X	X	X	X	X	
68	Cowboy's Delight	F		X	X		X	X	X	X
69	Spitfire Cycle	H		X	X			X	X	X
70	MacLean's Attack	H		X	X	X	X	X	X	X

Foreword

Whether dekeing a goalie in the crease or going top shelf with a snap shot, attacking and scoring are keys to winning hockey. When given an opportunity to score, you must take advantage of it. When there seems no opportunity to score, you must create it.

Goal scoring stats can be misleading. Your percentage of goals scored versus shots on goal is a function of much more than shooting skill and accuracy. For example, one season I took 397 shots and make 52 goals (13%), and another year I took 232 shots and scored 51 goals (22%). Were my shooting skills that much better in one season than the other? On paper, yes. In reality, no.

Scoring takes great technique and accuracy, but it also takes an aggressive attitude, good decision making, and opportunities resulting from solid team play. A player with a great shot won't get the puck in the net without the total scoring package. In this book, Newell Brown and Vern Stenlund show you how to develop both the technical skills and the attitude to be a big-time scorer.

If *Hockey Drills for Scoring* had been around when I was developing my offensive game, practice would have been more fun, and I probably would have scored a few more goals along the way. Brown and Stenlund know their stuff. If you want to improve your ability to attack the net, take their advice and take their book to practice. It's a scoring opportunity you can't pass up.

Brendan Shanahan

To our families in thanks for all their support during our hockey coaching exploits. To Lori, Erika, and Adam Brown, and to Lynne, Laura, Kara, Erik, and Tyler Stenlund, we truly appreciate your sacrifices through the years. We love you all.

Acknowledgments

The authors wish to express their appreciation to several individuals and organizations who helped make the publication of this book a reality. We wish to thank the people at I-Tech for supplying high-quality hockey equipment for our photo sessions that detailed specific skill techniques. We also wish to thank Wayne and the entire staff at South Windsor Arena for allowing us to use their fine facility for photo shoots. We would like to extend special thanks to our photographer, Gerry Marentette, a player himself who has a great eye for hockey photography. Kudos to all those at Huron Hockey who continue to support coaches in these types of publishing ventures, and to Tony Farias and Jason Wilson, the two players who demonstrated most of the shooting sequences, as well as Rob Belleau who handled the goal tending duties for the photo shoot. And finally to all the people at Human Kinetics, including Ted Miller, Kirby Mittelmeier, and Jennifer Stallard—thanks again for keeping the process moving forward.

Introduction

When you think about the thrilling moments in sports, what comes to mind? In baseball it might be the classic duel between pitcher and hitter: two out in the bottom of the ninth, with the winning run at the plate. In football perhaps it is the quarterback, with only seconds to play, heaving a long bomb to deliver the winning touchdown. In hockey certainly it would be a one-on-one confrontation between goaltender and shooter off a breakaway down the ice.

Offense has always lent a drama to sport, bringing fans to their feet and making even the most veteran players weak in the knees. *Hockey Drills for Scoring* is designed to help aspiring players and coaches develop this exciting aspect of play. Whether it's a long slap shot that finds the back of the net or a fancy move that confounds the opposing goalie, scoring represents a fundamental aspect of hockey requiring skill, which means practicing and refining.

This book will provide you, the player or coach, with practical suggestions to help master scoring skills. From learning how to properly execute a specific kind of scoring shot to developing the ability to redirect a puck on the net, or for simply understanding how to position yourself for better scoring chances, *Hockey Drills for Scoring* has the types of information that proficient, modern players use to improve their scoring. By practicing the drills and concepts presented here, players can learn to master scoring fundamentals and make them an integral part of their game.

Mastering the 70 shooting and scoring drills in this book will help you because the activities are designed to develop practical skills that relate directly to game situations. You will immediately see benefits from the drills in the competitive games you play—just as coaches at the Huron Hockey School have seen over the years as they developed these special methods of teaching scoring skills.

Players and coaches alike will find the drills in this book a valuable resource for planning both individual and group practice sessions. Moreover, the activities are useful at many different levels of coaching. They benefit players from the youngest beginner to the most experienced all-star. The basic skills really never change . . . but the ability to execute these skills must develop!

Hockey Drills for Scoring is more than just another "drill" book. It includes tips and ideas for each activity to help players and coaches focus on the important aspects of skill development, dramatically reducing the time required to master specific skills.

How the Book Is Organized

The drills have been assembled with some specific organizational objectives. For example, rather than combining drills from all phases of the game of hockey, this book focuses on one major aspect of play, namely moving toward a high level of skill in scoring. We wanted to avoid a pitfall that many coaches and players encounter with many books, videos, hockey seminars, or clinics crammed with a variety of drills. Armed with a wealth of new information, coaches and players go home ready to conquer the world. They inevitably discover, unfortunately, that many instructional materials are overly complicated and lack appropriate drills for their specific skill level. Often the result is confusion and frustration for everyone involved.

To provide a useful and meaningful resource instead, this book does not attempt to provide drills for all situations—the game of hockey is far too complex. It offers varied and flexible drills focused on scoring but also incorporating other aspects of the game as a part of scoring activities. To design an effective practice session, coaches and players then select the specific objectives to emphasize for each particular drill.

Most of the key elements associated with shooting and goal scoring receive detailed drill through the activities in this book. Individual chapters focus on key components of shooting and scoring, allowing both players and coaches to better understand the principles and drilling sequences for each important section. Whether you need to improve one-time shooting ability, gain insight as to high percentage shooting angles, learn to score under pressure, or simply work more on basic shooting technique, this book allows for immediate improvement. We examine the most vital components of this important hockey skill in detail through drills that produce results.

This book also presents a level of progression from simple activities at the beginning of each chapter to more difficult drills at the end of each chapter. In assembling the drills for this book we gave special attention to providing simple activities that beginners will almost immediately find doable, allowing players at any level to achieve a measure of success. We supplied guidelines for refining each drill to present more experienced players with a greater challenge. We called these "Drill Progressions." Often we increased the difficulty by changing time and space parameters, adding pressure to the drills, or intensifying techniques. As players' skills increase, so too will their ability to execute the activities at a faster pace. They will know their scoring skills have improved because they will be able to perform the tasks more quickly and accurately. The results will be obvious—the puck will be in the net more often!

As you peruse the individual drills in this book, pay special attention to the "Key Points" section of each activity. It contains suggestions to assist you in perfecting the drills and making skill learning more effective. Years of teaching and coaching experience have gone into developing these activities, and the comments that accompany them reflect the approaches of the many coaches who have come through the Huron hockey program, many of whom have reached the professional level. Their advice will serve you well as you continue along the road to mastery.

On a larger scale the same philosophy of progression applies, with each succeeding chapter of the book offering more challenging activities. This progression affords a wider range of players and coaches with practical and useful material, regardless of skill level. Progressions are also seen at the end of individual drills where additional suggestions provide ways to alter an activity. By changing some of the parameters of individual drills you not only add difficulty but also add variety! You may notice that many of the suggestions for the drill progressions involve physical contact as a way of affecting both the time and space that players have available for completing an activity. We recommend that you determine which of these contact activities are appropriate to your players' age or skill level before implementing them in a practice format.

Few of the drills require extra equipment or substantial set-up time. Most need only a stick, a puck, and some ice. As a result, they can be done without wasting time and effort; you can spend valuable ice time doing the activities, not discussing them.

Many of the drills are half-ice activities. This means that coaches may choose to run the same drill simultaneously on both halves of the ice sheet. You might choose to practice two *different* drills simultaneously, perhaps a specific type of drill on one half of the ice that is reinforced through another activity. You will see that many of the half-ice drills show an additional drill progression, meaning that often you are receiving two drills instead of one. This uses ice time effectively, especially at the minor levels where practice costs and availability are at a premium. With half-ice drills, teams can accomplish double the practice effect over the same period of time.

We often incorporate some form of line formation in drills involving groups of three players. This drilling technique has advantages for both players and coaches: First, it decreases wasted ice time, using less relocation of personnel during practice. A practice could be run in its entirety using this format. Second, line drills become an identifiable feature of practice that players can easily adapt to given specific changes from activity to activity. Coaches lay a foundation for drill practice. Newer drill variations and progressions then may be readily added, because the players are already familiar with the basic drilling flow. In addition, players who work regularly with common line mates will become better acquainted with each one's strengths and weaknesses, their timing, and their shot preferences. The result is more successful and confident players.

At the end of the book you will find sample practice plans showing how to integrate the drills into practice sessions. To make planning your practices easier and more flexible, go to the Drill Finder, an index-type section that will help you identify other aspects of play used in specific drills that might fill the needs of your specific situation.

Hockey Drills for Scoring is packed with information that will help you become a more consistent goal scorer. Top-level coaches agree that the trademark of a true goal scorer is the ability to get the job done on a regular, consistent basis. By first understanding the key concepts in this book and then practicing long and hard, you will have an opportunity to become a consistent producer. Good luck as you begin to master the skills in this book.

Roller Hockey

The types of activities and drilling sequences in this book are also suitable for roller hockey, a sport closely related to ice hockey. Roller players and coaches can easily adapt many of the drills to a non-ice environment. It's important to recognize, however, that certain skills may be affected by factors such as increased friction and different playing materials. If you intend to incorporate some of the ice hockey drills into your roller hockey practice, simply try the drill and modify it as necessary. Any problems you might encounter will quickly become evident, and you can then make adjustments.

Key to Diagrams

X or O	Player/opposing player/pair of players
(C/L)	Coach or leader
D	Defenseman
F	Forward
(G)	Goaltender
⟶	Forward skating
⋯⋯⋯⟶	Forward skating with puck
— ·· — ··⟶	Backward skating
— • — • ⟶	Backward skating with puck
‖ or =	Stopping
⟋◯⟍	Turns
⟋○⟍	Tight turns
⟋◠◠⟍	Pivots (forward to backward, backward to forward)
- - - - - ⟶	Passing
⟹	Shooting
⟋◟◞⟶	Deke
⟶⟨	Deflection or redirect
⟶⟨S	Screen
⋰⋱	Pucks
△	Pylons (or cones)
⟺	Hockey stick

1 Becoming an Effective Scorer

Anyone who plays hockey enjoys the thrill of releasing a shot that finds the back of the net for a goal. Scoring is an exciting part of the game, and most players continually work to improve their skills in this area. Some basic concepts—from stick selection to proper positioning of your body and the puck—should be considered to maximize your chances of becoming a more successful offensive player. The first part of this chapter examines these basic concepts. The second part details four major principles that you should refer to often while developing proper shooting technique and mechanics. By learning the concepts and practicing the principles provided, your improvement in both shooting and scoring technique and production can become a reality.

Basic Shooting and Scoring Concepts

To become a more successful scorer, you should first examine the basic how-tos of selecting a stick, positioning your body and the puck, using your legs, and following through. Although some of this information might seem simple to those who have had a lot of hockey experience, it is nevertheless wise to review these points, making sure that you have not forgotten some simple yet key concepts.

Selecting a Stick

Choosing the proper stick is a key part of effective shooting; unfortunately, there is no single correct formula—it is in large part a process of trial and error. We recommend that players experiment by exchanging sticks with teammates during practice. Exchanging sticks is an inexpensive way of discovering which stick has the right "feel" for you. Even professional players will occasionally try swapping sticks with a teammate, especially when mired in a scoring slump.

1

Along with trying out different sticks, there are a few points about stick design and construction you should be aware of to help you decide which stick is right for you. Stick lie refers to the angle at which the shaft and blade portions of the stick come together. The higher the lie number, the more upright the stick will be when the blade is flat on the ice surface. This has implications given the different skating styles of players, some preferring a more upright position while skating and stick handling; others prefer a more crouched positions. Try to choose a stick lie compatible with your style.

Blade curvature can refer to either the amount of bend from the heel to the toe of the blade, or the curve that is often put in by players themselves from top to bottom that results in a "twisted" effect. We recommend a minimal amount of curvature for younger players until they can effectively control the effect that curve will impact on any given type of shot.

For stick shaft types, both composition and rigidity are quite variable. Newer materials such as aluminum, kevlar, graphite, and titanium now complement the traditional wood sticks available on the market. With so many options, players can select a stick that has the right amount of stiffness or rigidity given their particular needs and levels of strength. As a general rule, sticks that "give," or flex while shots are being taken, provide a whipping action that adds extra speed to the shot. Therefore, younger players not yet physically mature should use lighter, more flexible sticks to assist the shooting process. Only when you are older and able to generate more force at the point of contact with the puck should more rigid sticks be considered.

While stick length and lie, blade curvature, shaft rigidity, and stick composition are all factors that come into play, players must determine what works for them on an individual basis. If you are unsure of the type of stick you should be using, ask a coach to watch your shooting technique or have someone videotape you during a shooting and scoring sequence. Watching yourself on video is an excellent way to see how the length and the lie of your stick can affect shooting power and accuracy.

First, check to see that you're keeping the entire stick blade on the ice when shooting—an important element for good puck control. Not using the full blade might indicate that you have a stick that is at the wrong lie given your specific skating and shooting style. Is the stick so long that you are losing control of the puck before you ever get the shot off? Or do you often fan and miss the puck when shooting, perhaps the result of using an improper lie? Check that the stick length allows you to be comfortable when releasing a shot. If the stick is too long, you will not be able to control the puck with ease, and thus generating a quick release will be difficult. A stick that is too short will force you to shoot the puck from a position closer to the body, which could inhibit shot speed.

Another simple technique for checking whether all your stick blade is in contact with the ice surface while shooting is to look at the tape on the bottom of the blade. Do this after taking several shots and using the stick so that wear patterns become apparent. If the heel (back) or toe (front) section of the blade appears more worn than the rest of the blade, you may want to try a stick with a different lie. Trial and error will allow you to find the proper stick for your individual style, strengths, and weaknesses.

One final consideration in stick selection is the stiffness of the shaft. As a general rule, the stiffer the shaft of the stick, the more strength and power a player must possess to generate puck speed. We suggest that younger players use sticks that have more flexible shafts, which will assist in generating faster shots. A more flexible shaft allows for a "whipping" action at the point of contact with the ice and puck, resulting in additional shot speed. With a very stiff shaft, this whipping action is more difficult to achieve. As you gain more strength and confidence in your shot-making ability, you may want to switch to a stiffer shaft. Try different sticks to see which one works best for you.

Loading the Cannon

"Loading the cannon" is an expression that has been used over the years at Huron Hockey School by instructors when they teach players how to prepare for all shots. Loading the cannon refers to proper hand location on the stick shaft to execute an effective shot. By loading, or sliding your bottom hand down the shaft of the stick, you are locking into a power position for shooting.

One way to emphasize this point is to first attempt a shot while keeping your hands close together on the stick. Shooting the puck with the hands close together makes any shot difficult to complete. Lowering the bottom hand gives greater control and power (see figure 1.1).

The most accurate and the hardest shooters will turn their wrists over when shooting: the bottom hand moves from a palm-up position in preparation for the shot to a palm-down position as the shot is completed at the follow-through stage, while the top hand on the stick works in exactly the opposite fashion. Coaches often demonstrate this concept by removing their playing gloves and having players watch the action at the wrists during a shooting exercise (see figures 1.2a and 1.2b).

FIGURE 1.1   Load the cannon by sliding the bottom hand lower on the stick shaft.

By demonstrating the technique, coaches are able to better assist players in understanding that wrists must turn over during shooting. Also, it reinforces the concept that fingers and fingertips, not the palm of the hand, control the stick. This allows for greater feel of the puck and more accuracy of the shot, especially in goal-scoring situations in which finesse and control are often as important as the speed of the shot.

Positioning for the Shot

Much like hitting a golf ball, shooting a puck must become a skill that is easily replicated time after time. To help develop accurate repetition, proper positioning of the puck during the shot is essential, both in relation to your body and to the placement of the stick blade. Consider the following tips.

• **Be Conscious of Puck Position Relative to Your Body**

Try to keep the arms out and away from the hips when shooting so that maximum leverage and power can be achieved, resulting in a

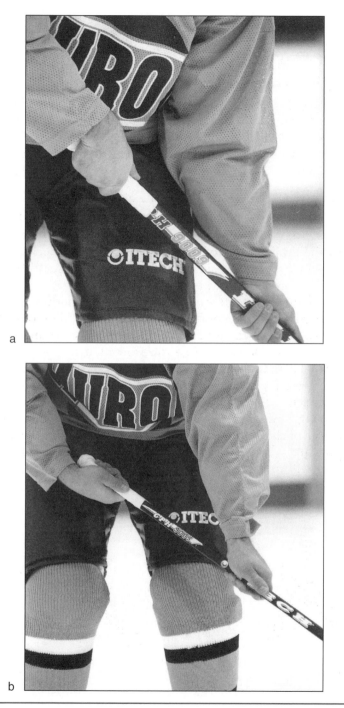

FIGURE 1.2   For best technique, your wrists should turn over during the shot.

faster and harder shot. This position permits you to look out and down, not just down. Looking out or ahead during shooting helps you locate your target.

- **Keep the Puck in the Center of the Blade at Point of Impact**

  To use a golf analogy, if a ball leaves the club face off the heel or toe rather than from the middle of the club, both accuracy and distance will be affected. The same result occurs when a puck is released from the wrong part of the blade. The shot will either hook or slice off-target and will lack the necessary speed to be considered effective.

- **Release the Puck Near the Midline of the Body**

  Imagine the shot consisting of three zones as pictured in figure 1.3. Zone 1 is a preparatory area where the puck begins its path. Zone 2, or the midline area of the body, is where the puck should be situated when you release the shot. Zone 3 represents the follow-through phase after the puck is released.

  The midline area refers to an imaginary line dividing the body in half lengthwise from your head down; the puck should be close to this imaginary line as your shot is released. This imaginary line lies in front of your body any time you are stationary or moving along a parallel path to the net that forces you to shoot across your body. When in full flight and heading directly toward your intended target, the puck will be at the side of the body, and the midline passes down your side profile instead. In either scenario, you should not drag the puck past this midline area because in doing so leverage, power, and accuracy will be compromised. By shooting from Zone 2, you will use maximum weight distribution while having the greatest possible control of your shot.

Zone 1   Zone 2   Zone 3

FIGURE 1.3   Zone 1 for preparation, Zone 2 for release, Zone 3 for follow-through

- **Use the Ice as a Springboard for Faster Shots**
  You should attempt to hit just behind the puck on the ice when releasing a shot. This will help generate shot speed by creating a momentary whipping action in the stick shaft, which increases speed as the stick blade contacts the puck.

  To develop this skill, you will need to shoot down on the puck, as opposed to trying to pick the puck clean off the ice surface. Using our golf example again, you should not try to shoot a puck as if your stick were a pitching wedge, looking to deftly chip a ball out of the rough or sand. Rather, think of your stick as a driver. In hockey, your "driver" is going to make contact with the ice before reaching the puck. Over time you will begin to see the improvement in shot speed as this skill is mastered.

Using Your Legs

When you watch a great baseball pitcher deliver the ball to home plate, you might presume that the arm is responsible for the speed of the ball. This is true only in part, for the real power behind the pitch is generated through the big muscle groups in the legs and torso. The momentum developed by the legs and torso helps to put speed on the ball. The same principle applies for increasing the speed of the puck in hockey—the fastest shots begin with the legs.

We recommend that you constantly work on bending the knees closer to 90 degrees when shooting so that these big muscle groups can give the greatest possible assistance to your shooting (see figure 1.4). By driving forward and through with the back leg as your shot is initiated, extra speed and force are generated. As you execute the shot, your body weight should be transferred to the lead, or front, leg so that both muscle power and body mass (weight) contribute most effectively. We'll look more closely at shooting technique in chapter 2.

Following Through

The trajectory of the puck and where the puck ends up will always be affected by the follow-through of the stick as the puck is released to its target. As a general rule, the higher the follow-through, the higher the shot. This has great implications for scoring situations. For example, as a puck carrier draws closer to the goaltender, most coaches would advise that the shot be directed into the top portions of the net because many goalies begin to drop down as the shooter approaches. Using a higher follow-through will assist you in getting the puck up and over the goalie.

FIGURE 1.4   Knee bend is vital to shooting properly.

Conversely, from farther distances you'll often want to keep the puck lower so that the goalie will be forced to move his or her feet to make the save. Lower shots will require that shooters make a conscious effort to follow through with a lower trajectory.

Shooting and Scoring Principles

The concepts we just described provide an important foundation for developing proper shooting mechanics. Players should continually remember, review, and refine these skills. We now turn to the next set of principles or building blocks that you will need to understand to improve your shooting technique as a means of scoring goals: identifying the target area, developing a quick release, positioning away from the puck, and following your shot to the net.

Principle #1: Identify Your Target Area

"The Great One," Wayne Gretzky, once noted that when shooting to score, he sees beyond the goaltender to open areas and shoots to hit the net meshing in one of those open areas. He attempts to block out the goalie and works instead at identifying a target within the net to aim for. Well, if it's good enough for Wayne, it probably should be good enough for all of us! By focusing on technique and shot selection instead of on the goalie, you are removing one more distraction that could affect the outcome of your shot. Although you must be aware of the goalie's position, the key to scoring goals is as much knowing where he *isn't,* because that is where you will find the opening for a goal.

Shooters should be aware of five key goal-scoring areas. You must first identify the best option among these five while preparing to shoot, then direct the puck toward the best option. In figure 1.5, we see two areas in the lower portions of the net, two areas up high, and one location commonly referred to as "the 5-Hole," which is between the goalie's leg pads. Effective goal scorers understand where potential openings are and will be as a play develops.

Principle #2: Develop a Quick Release

Ideally, every shot you take should be from a position where maximum weight transfer and knee bend can be applied to achieve the most accurate

FIGURE 1.5 Five areas for scoring goals

and hardest shot possible. Unfortunately, most shots taken during a typical game occur under the pressures of time and space, meaning that players must learn to shoot off either foot, a difficult skill indeed.

Developing a quick release means that you must be able to shoot the puck in less-than-ideal circumstances, but, just as important, it also implies that the decision-making process must be sped up as well. Mark Messier might be the ultimate example of a professional player who can release the puck quickly, off either foot and from nearly any position in the offensive zone, when the pressure is on. Experienced goal scorers like Messier eventually realize that the quickness with which the shot is released is a key variable to success in goal scoring, even more important than the hardness of the shot.

The ability to catch the defender and goalie off-balance through quick release, using the element of surprise, is a definite advantage for would-be goal scorers. The longer you hold on to the puck before shooting, the longer the goaltender has to prepare for your shot.

To reduce shooting angles and goal-scoring opportunities, many goalies use a technique commonly referred to as telescoping (see figure 1.6a). This action refers to a goaltender moving out and away from the goal crease area in an attempt to stop a shot. Goalies who do a lot of telescoping are attempting to reduce the amount of space that the shooter will have to work with (figure 1.6b). Obviously, the smaller the openings to shoot at, the more perfect your shots will have to be. Telescoping can be a powerful tool for goaltenders if properly used.

By releasing the puck quickly, shooters will inhibit a goalie's ability to telescope, which in turn increases goal-scoring opportunities. In addition, a quick release might catch a goalie moving into this telescoping mode, which means that the goaltender's feet are in motion. When this occurs, you receive another benefit because it is very difficult for a goaltender to move the legs left or right when moving out or toward the attacking player. The ultimate form of quick release—one-time shooting, in which the attacker shoots the puck almost as quickly as he receives it—will be detailed later in the book.

Principle #3: Position Yourself Properly Away From the Puck

Playing away from the puck in the context of shooting and scoring means preparing yourself to receive a puck in shooting situations. Whenever you are in the offensive zone and your team has puck possession, try to move into areas where the puck can be passed to you for executing a high-percentage shot. Much as a wide receiver in football looks for

a

b

FIGURE 1.6   When shooters delay their shots, goaltenders have time to telescope (b), reducing goal-scoring opportunities.

"seams" in the defensive secondary to exploit, you should constantly be in motion on the attack to position yourself where the puck can be delivered to you cleanly. Most great goal scorers understand this principle and constantly try to position themselves in such a way that scoring opportunities are maximized.

Body and stick positioning are also important: players preparing to receive a puck should be positioned with their stick blade on the ice and have the passer and goalie in their field of view. These positions allow players to see both the puck and the goalie position and get the shot off quickly. After all, it would be difficult for even the greatest goal scorers to execute their shots consistently if their backs are turned to the play. The principle of preparing to receive the puck in shooting and scoring situations is often a key factor in separating high-production goal scorers from the rest of the pack.

Principle #4: Always Follow Your Shot to the Net

Following your initial shot to the net for rebound opportunities is often the most neglected of the four main principles yet can result in many easy shots and goal-scoring opportunities. Even the greatest hockey players often fail to move toward the net after taking a shot on-target, the result being that rebound chances can be cleared by the goalie or defensemen. At elite levels of play, first-shot goals become rare prizes and rebounds account for a higher percentage of total goals scored. Yet many players continue to turn away from the net, perhaps heading to the corner of the rink after taking a first shot on-target. This principle should be drilled through effective practice with activities that reinforce the importance of going to the net for "garbage goals" that result off rebound opportunities.

Although the preceding concepts and principles are basic for many players, they are nevertheless often forgotten, even by professional players, during the heat of battle. If you are struggling with your shooting or are in a prolonged scoring drought, revisit the key points in this chapter. You might be surprised at how these insights will affect your results in a positive way!

© Casey B. Gibson

Shooting Fundamentals

In this chapter, we will examine and describe the four basic hockey shots—the wrist shot, the snap shot, the slap shot, and the backhand shot—by looking at the mechanics of each through the three zones mentioned in chapter 1: preparation, release, and follow-through. The accompanying drills may then be used to reinforce proper technique and mechanics for all four shots.

For younger players, proper mechanics are more important than successful outcomes. Often, youngsters who are not physically mature enough to raise the puck will forget fundamentals and try to "hit the glass" by lifting rather than shooting the puck, which will not help them develop shooting skills in the long run. Coaches should reinforce the ideas that time and strength will take care of outcomes and that players must first build a solid foundation of mechanics in shooting a puck—mechanics such as those discussed and demonstrated through photos in this chapter.

Much as the professional golfer will practice a proper golf swing that holds up at "crunch time," so too must hockey players possess sound shooting technique that can withstand pressure as the clock winds down and the heat is turned up during a game. By mastering these four basic shots, players will be able to shoot from virtually anywhere on the ice and improve their chances of scoring. The drills in this chapter are de-signed to reinforce these skills at an entry level.

The four basic shots in hockey possess similar fundamental mechan-ics relative to puck and body positions as detailed in chapter 1:

- Locate the puck close to the midblade area for maximum accuracy.
- Release the puck from Zone 2, generally at a point no farther for-ward than the lead, or front, skate.
- Concentrate on bending the knees to ensure the hardest shot possible.
- Slide the bottom hand lower on the stick shaft to "load the cannon."
- Complete the shot by following through to the intended target.

In addition, each shot has some unique characteristics that must be learned, understood, and then applied through practice. Let's take a closer look at each shot, starting with the wrist shot.

15

Wrist Shot

The wrist shot is the most basic of all hockey shots and gives maximal control. This is because the puck remains in contact with the stick blade for the longest time possible, giving you more time to control exactly when the shot should be released and where you want it to go. Players who properly master the wrist shot are able to keep their eyes on the target and not on the puck, a definite advantage for potential scorers.

Zone 1: The puck does not leave your stick blade in this zone (figure 2.1a). Drag the puck through Zone 1 with your body weight distributed mostly on the back leg. Remember the basics: keep the puck in the midblade area and load the cannon.

Zone 2: Weight should shift toward your front, or lead, leg as the puck is pulled through Zone 2 (figure 2.1b). Flex the stick shaft by putting downward pressure on the stick blade into the ice surface. The puck can roll slightly from the heel to the midblade area before the release point.

Zone 3: Stick blade should be pointing at target area, like pointing a finger (figure 2.1c). You should be able to see the back side of the stick blade once the shot has been completed. Weight should be totally transferred to the front leg.

FIGURE 2.1a   Preparation

FIGURE 2.1b   Release

FIGURE 2.1c   Follow-through

Snap Shot

The snap shot is the shot of choice among many professional players because it takes less time to release to the target. Because the snap shot gets most of its power from the wrists and arms, it can be completed off either foot once you have sufficient strength. This shot is the money, or "kill," shot in hockey and is often used in tight situations when you need to fire off a quick shot.

Zone 1: The stick blade and the puck are not in contact in this zone (figure 2.2a). Rather, the stick is slightly pulled back as you prepare to "snap" at the puck, as opposed to pulling it through this zone. Weight is evenly distributed across both legs.

Zone 2: The stick blade will hit the ice up to six inches directly behind the puck (figure 2.2b). Hitting the ice surface will increase the snapping effect. The wrists must turn over quickly or snap as the puck is contacted. This will add speed to the shot, but it requires sound technique and strong wrists to properly execute.

Zone 3: Similar to the wrist shot in that you must point the stick blade toward the target, but you will often not have enough time to complete a full follow-through (figure 2.2c). The follow-through will be quick and relatively short.

FIGURE 2.2a   Preparation

FIGURE 2.2b   Release

FIGURE 2.2c   Follow-through

Slap Shot

The glamour shot in hockey is the slap shot, but it requires considerable time and practice to control. It is generally regarded as the least accurate but fastest of all shot types. This shot is often deflected or blocked by opponents because of the longer setup time.

Zone 1: The technique is the same as for a snap shot in that no contact will be made with the puck through this zone (figure 2.3a). The stick shaft is drawn back and held above the waist, sometimes above head level. The weight is evenly distributed across both skates. For a slap shot, the cannon should really be loaded up!

Zone 2: The torso twists, assisting in creating torque, force, and finally speed (figure 2.3b). The blade should hit the ice behind the puck initially, just as it does for the snap shot. Weight will shift dramatically to the front leg and skate as impact is made.

Zone 3: Coming out of this shot, you should almost feel like you are going to fall, so extreme is the weight transfer from the back leg to the front (figure 2.3c). The stick should stay low when attempting to keep the puck down, but come through higher if the shooter is looking to hit the upper portions of the net. The shoulder drives through toward the intended target to maximize the speed of your shot.

FIGURE 2.3a   Preparation

FIGURE 2.3b   Release

FIGURE 2.3c   Follow-through

The Backhand Shot

Many goaltenders maintain that the backhand shot is the most difficult shot to judge. Often underused even at the pro levels, the backhand can be an effective offensive weapon, especially when players do not have the time to switch to the more favored forehand position.

Zone 1: The puck should be closer to the heel of the blade for this shot because of the curvature of most sticks (figure 2.4a). You get more control by keeping the puck farther back on the blade. Your weight should be loaded on the back, or push, leg and the lower hand slides down the shaft just as with the wrist shot.

Zone 2: Turn the toes of the lead foot toward the intended target as release is started (figure 2.4b). This will "open" the hips and increase both speed and accuracy. Snap the wrists at the point of release. Power is generated from the muscles in the back leg and foot area as your weight is transferred toward the front leg. The entire upper body from the waist up turns.

Zone 3: Remember to follow through high for upper net locations or keep the stick blade lower and closer to the ice for a lower trajectory (figure 2.4c). The weight shifts forward and onto the front leg as the shot is completed.

FIGURE 2.4a   Preparation

FIGURE 2.4b Release

FIGURE 2.4c Follow-through

HIT THE TARGET

PURPOSE

- To introduce basic principles of proper shooting technique in a stationary format
- To assess shooting skill levels among players

EQUIPMENT None

TIME 3-5 minutes, depending on skill level

PROCEDURE — Half-Ice Drill

1. Players take a puck and position themselves 5 to 10 feet away from the boards anywhere around the ice surface.
2. On the whistle, players attempt the different shot types while aiming at a specific spot along the boards.
3. The coach can designate which shot to practice and whether to shoot with a high or low follow-through.

KEY POINTS

- Players shift weight toward the front leg as shots are released, which will maximize shot speed.
- Players should remember and practice the principles of shooting, concentrating on technique through the three zones of preparation, release, and follow-through.

DRILL PROGRESSIONS

- Have players attempt to hit the same spot five times consecutively before moving to another shot.
- Work with a partner who lays a stick along the ice, forcing the shooter to raise the puck (see diagram).
- Hang tires over the boards and have players shoot for the hole; have moving targets as skill improves.

HIT THE TARGET

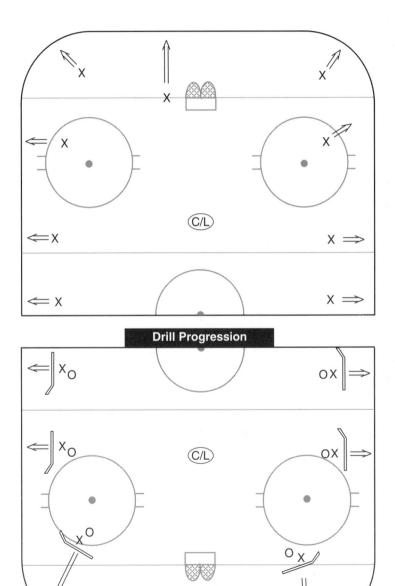

Drill Progression

② DEAD PUCK

PURPOSE

- To introduce basic shooting activities with a stationary puck
- To add movement by the player as a progression when shooting a stationary puck

EQUIPMENT   None

TIME   2-4 minutes

PROCEDURE — Half-Ice Drill

1. Players leave pucks in designated spots around the ice and skate toward them.
2. Attempts are made to shoot the stationary puck, using one of the four basic hockey shots, while players are in motion.
3. Retrieve the puck after each shot and set up for another turn.

KEY POINTS

- This drill will add movement, yet it reduces difficulty by allowing players to shoot a stationary puck.
- Players should concentrate on having: (a) proper hand location on stick; (b) arms away from hips; (c) entire blade of the stick on ice; (d) knees bent; (e) puck in midportion of the stick blade; and (f) body in motion.
- Coaches can circulate to assist players where needed.

DRILL PROGRESSIONS

- Do sets of three shots in a row consecutively, where the player skates a small circle after shooting and returns for succeeding shots (see diagram).
- Have players count the number of times they can raise the puck or hit a specific target.
- Turn this into a team activity and attempt to beat the previous total compiled by all team members combined.

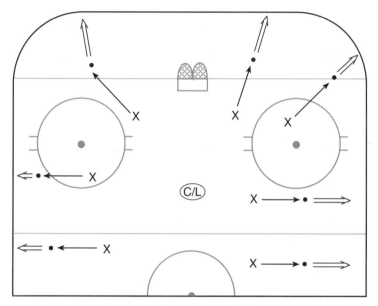

Drill Progression

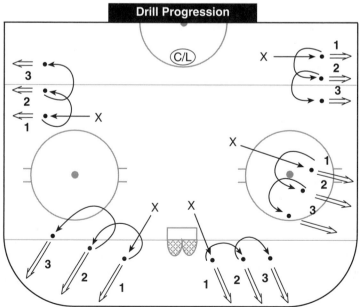

③ TARGET BOARD

PURPOSE

- To reinforce proper mechanics in attempting to raise a puck

EQUIPMENT   Boards of different heights, from 1 inch and higher, long enough to extend post to post across the goal mouth area.

TIME   2-4 minutes

PROCEDURE — Half-Ice Drill

1. The coach or helper lays a board across the goal crease from goal post to goal post, covering the entire ice area between the two points while leaving a portion of the net open.
2. Players assemble in a semicircle and one at a time attempt to raise the puck over the board into the net.
3. Once all players have had a turn, they each retrieve their puck and return for another set.
4. Sets of shots can be released from varying distances from the net at the coach's discretion.

KEY POINTS

- Players must be reminded to try not to pick the puck up off the ice in an attempt to raise it. Rather, proper mechanics should be reinforced, such as using the three shooting zones, loading the cannon, and so on.
- Watch for "lazy arms" (hands and arms too close to the body). Keeping hands and arms away from the body while shooting helps players to eventually raise the puck.

DRILL PROGRESSIONS

- Leave the pucks stationary and have players skate toward them, which will add speed to their shot (see diagram).
- Use a board that has one end higher than the other. Dependent on skill levels, players can choose which end of the board to shoot for, making this a more inclusive activity in which most players can be successful.

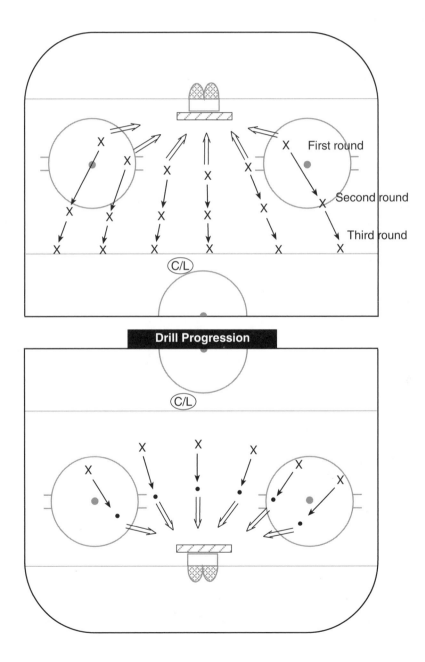

First round

Second round

Third round

C/L

Drill Progression

C/L

4 THE COMBO

PURPOSE

- To practice the four shot types in succession
- To introduce shooting with puck control and motion

EQUIPMENT   None

TIME   3-5 minutes

PROCEDURE — Full-Ice Drill

1. Players are in two equal groups, one each at the blue lines on either side of the rink. Pucks are at both blue lines.
2. When the whistle blows, players in both lines move one at a time toward the goaltender and release a shot on net, then skate hard to the far blue line, retrieve a puck, and wait for the next whistle.
3. The coach will designate which shot to take and will vary shot from set to set.
4. Continue for a minimum of four sets to include all major shot types.

KEY POINTS

- Players should shoot and then skate hard out of the end, simulating a backchecking sequence.
- Goaltenders should challenge the shooters by telescoping (coming out of the crease area).
- Remember to practice this drill in both directions by starting the activity from the opposite side of the rink.

DRILL PROGRESSIONS

- Begin the drill with backward skating, forcing players to pivot forward before shooting.
- Increase the rate of whistle changes, forcing players to react more quickly.
- Add a deke sequence by slowing down the drill and having players attempt to fake a shot and move close to the goaltender for an in-tight move.

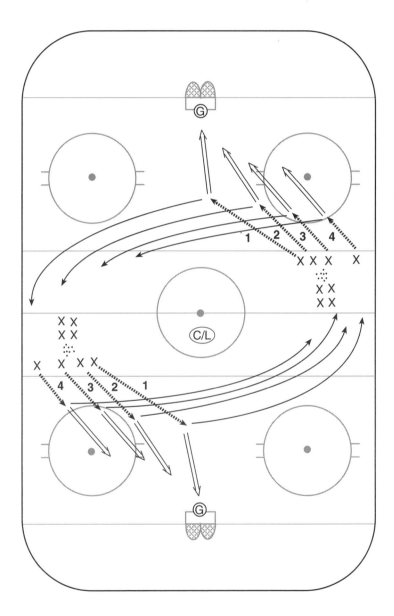

THE WAVE

PURPOSE

- To reinforce basic shooting technique

EQUIPMENT   None

TIME   2-4 minutes

PROCEDURE — Half-Ice Drill

1. Players are in equal groups, three groups per half, located near the center red line. Each group has pucks available for every skater.
2. Both ends go on the coach's whistle, with lines designated as first shooter, second shooter, and third shooter.
3. Once player from line one has begun to shoot, the second shooter moves toward the net for the second shot, followed by shooter three. Line one players go to back of line two, the line two players move to line three, and line three players go to the back of line one once their shots are taken.
4. Goalie must set a proper angle, make a save, then quickly move to prepare for ensuing shots.

KEY POINTS

- Players must time this drill so that the goalie has barely enough time to come across and properly position for the next shot.
- Players should be careful not to shoot if a goalie is injured by the preceding shot or is not fully attentive.

DRILL PROGRESSIONS

- Move from slow- to fast-paced timing as shooters and goalies establish a rhythm.
- Vary the shot selection with one line taking wrist shots, another snap shots, and so on.
- Alternate sides and finish with the middle line, forcing goalie to move from one side of the net across to the far side while under pressure (see diagram).

THE WAVE  5

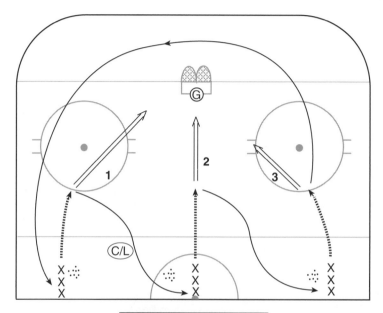

Drill Progression

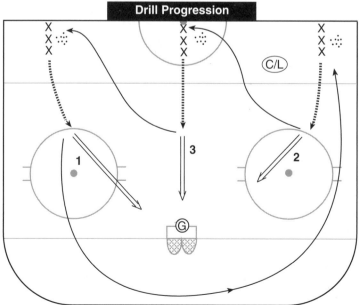

6 CIRCLE SHOTS

PURPOSE

- To provide players with a confined area in which to work on quick release while shooting

EQUIPMENT   None

TIME   2-3 minutes

PROCEDURE — Half-Ice Drill

1. Players take positions in one of four groups in the corners near the goal line.
2. On the whistle, a player from one line skates with the puck around the top of the face-off circle and releases a shot toward the goalie before reaching the hash mark area.
3. When the first player is at the midpoint of the face-off circle, a player from the other corner begins to skate a similar route from the opposite corner.
4. After shooting, players skate to the back of the opposite line.

KEY POINTS

- It is important for players to time their departures so that the goalie has a chance to set up for the shot.
- This drill moves quickly, so shooters and goalies must be alert. Players should gather any stray pucks and bring them back to the lines.

DRILL PROGRESSIONS

- Use a player from the opposite line as a passer.
- Add a second puck from the coach, which will be a second-shot opportunity.
- Advanced players should add pivots, backward skating, and other more difficult actions as they leave their line and move in for the shot (see diagram).

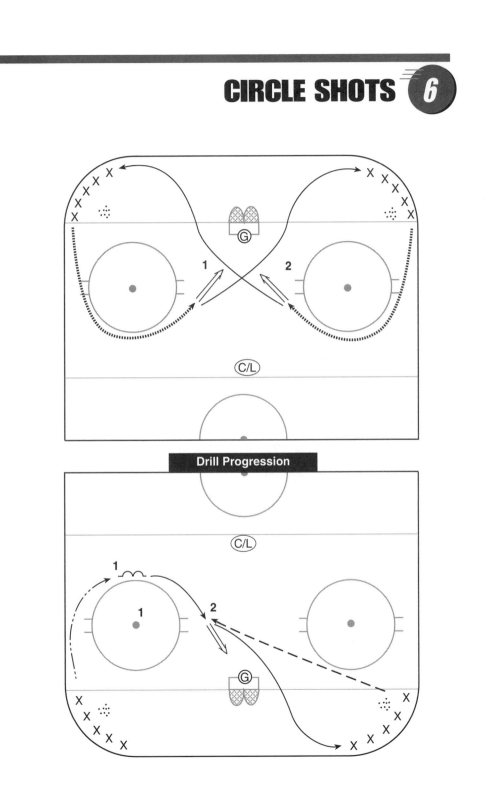

Drill Progression

⑦ TWO-LINE STRAIGHT

PURPOSE

- To reinforce puck handling, passing, and shooting skills while skating either forward or backward

EQUIPMENT   None

TIME   3-5 minutes

PROCEDURE — Full-Ice Drill

1. Players form in one of two lines at one end of the rink, and one line has pucks.
2. One player from each line skates toward the far end of the rink, passing a puck as they go while staying close together, no more than 6 feet apart.
3. The player who has possession of the puck after the red line shoots on net, and both players follow for any rebounds.
4. When completed, players peel off to opposite sides of the rink, pivot to backward skating, and return to the back of whichever line they did not originate from during the first rush.

KEY POINTS

- Pairs of players should have enough room between them to ensure recovery time for goalie.
- Next pair begins once the two in front of them have passed the near blue line.
- Pass forehand when in the appropriate line, and pass backhand when in that particular group. Practice passing both ways during this drill.

DRILL PROGRESSIONS

- Increase tempo of drill and passing distance (up to 20 feet).
- Have players begin by skating backward, then pivoting forward to take a shot and return to line.
- Add a backchecker to introduce pressure to the drill.

TWO-LINE STRAIGHT 7

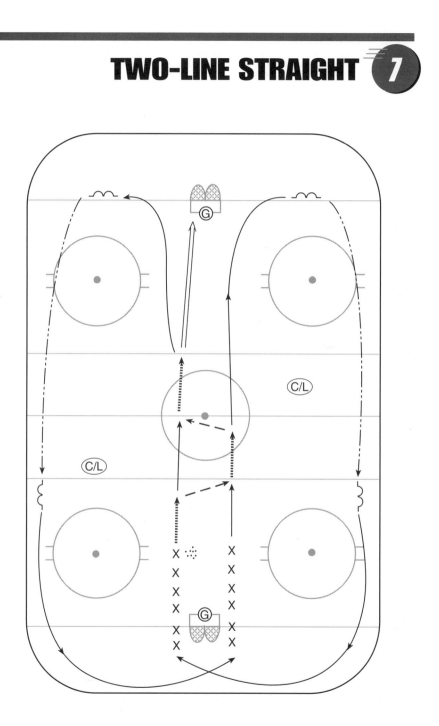

8 NUMBERS GAME

PURPOSE

- To force players into puck-control situations that call on basic skills
- To include a conditioning factor

EQUIPMENT   None

TIME   3-5 minutes

- Six repetitions maximum

PROCEDURE — Full-Ice Drill

1. Players are stationary on the ice in two equal groups at either end of the rink. Each player is assigned a number and has a puck.
2. Whenever the coach calls a number, the corresponding player skates forward and shoots on the goalie.
3. After shooting and following for any rebound, the shooter then proceeds to skate a full lap around the rink and returns to the original group at a different location in the zone.
4. The coach continues calling numbers until all players have completed six repetitions.
5. Coach may designate a specific shot to be used during each set.

KEY POINTS

- Keep drill high tempo, beginning the next repetition as soon as the previous one is concluded.
- This drill forces goalies to pick up movement from both the front and periphery.
- Players must watch for "oncoming traffic" when skating their lap after the shot.

DRILL PROGRESSIONS

- Have players begin by pivoting or turning before taking their shot on net.
- Demand higher speed and add pivots or turns throughout the route skated after the shot.
- For more advanced levels, have players from both ends exchange pucks by passing across the ice while doing their skating portion of the drill.

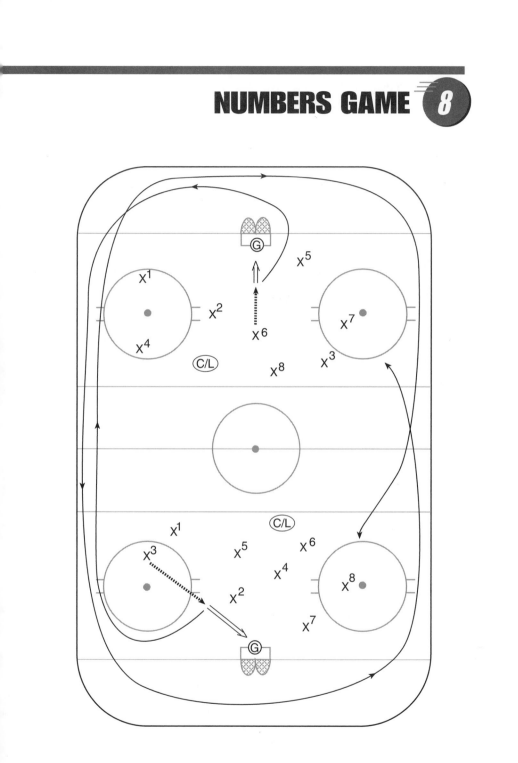

FULL-ICE LOOP

PURPOSE

- To reinforce proper edge control and turning technique while practicing basic shooting fundamentals

EQUIPMENT   None

TIME   2-4 minutes

PROCEDURE — Full-Ice Drill

1. Players are in one of four groups in the corners of the rink.
2. Coach blows whistle, and a player from groups at opposite corners of the rink (groups designated as *A)* begin to skate toward the far face-off circle in the pattern shown.
3. Once the turns have been made, players retrieve a puck from the center face-off area and move in for a shot.
4. After shooting, players stay at the back of the line in the end in which the shot is taken. Next whistle, players from the other two groups *(B)* follow the same pattern and sequence.

KEY POINTS

- Players must keep both feet and hands moving at the same time.
- Don't glide in the turns; keep the legs moving at all times.
- Only two opposite lines go at once, and players should always finish at the opposite end from which they began the drill.

DRILLS PROGRESSIONS

- Increase number of pivots, tight turns, or changes of direction during the prescribed route.
- Have players work in pairs, with trailing partner harassing puck carrier in front by hitting the gloves and arms.

FULL-ICE LOOP 9

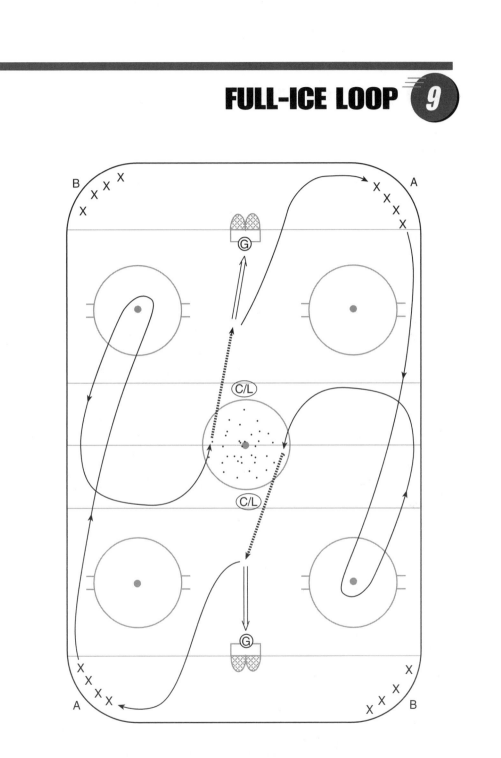

CENTER CUTS

PURPOSE

- To practice retrieving loose pucks and releasing quick shots from an angle
- For goalies to learn proper angling and telescoping technique

EQUIPMENT   None

TIME   4 minutes

PROCEDURE — Half-Ice Drill

1. Players are in the center face-off circle with pucks placed in four areas just inside the blue lines near the top of each face-off circle.
2. On the coach's whistle, two players skate in opposite directions around the circle as shown and move toward a puck, retrieve it, and take a shot on goal.
3. After shooting, players go to the goal line and skate hard back into the neutral zone while staying close to the boards.
4. Once shots are completed, the coach whistles the next pair to go in the opposite direction of the first pair, meaning that goalies at both ends will face shots from alternate sides.

KEY POINTS

- Shooters should move to retrieve pucks quickly and get the shot on-target without delay.
- Emphasize following the shot to the net for any rebounds.
- Goalies must attempt to restrict any short-side goals because angling is a fundamental objective for this activity. Short side refers to the side from which the shot is taken.

DRILL PROGRESSIONS

- Have coach pass a second puck from behind the net for in-tight shooting practice.
- Place a defender near the pucks; he or she will pick up the shooter as the puck is retrieved, forcing the attacker to get the shot on-target as quickly as possible.
- Have shooters cut to the middle to change shot angles, forcing goalies to react with their positioning.

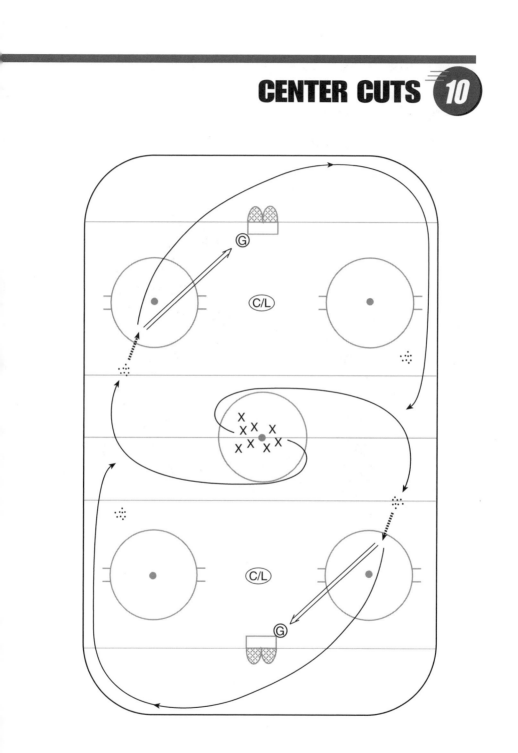

Scoring Angles

The ultimate reason for shooting the puck on net is to score a goal. Yet during a typical game at higher levels of play, the goaltenders might face 40 to 50 shots while only allowing two or three goals. Certainly the case could be made that the caliber of goaltending, as well as the quality of defensive pressure and increased speed of the game, improves at higher levels, which reduces the total number of goals scored.

Because of the lower shot-to-goal ratio at elite levels, players and coaches should ask themselves not only if there are certain higher-percentage scoring situations, but also what aspects of play define those situations. The angle at which the puck enters the goal area relative to the puck's position as the shot is taken certainly plays a role.

Factors Affecting Scoring Angles

Goals are often the result of minor discrepancies between the angles taken by the attacker versus the angles misplayed by the goaltender; therefore, understanding the importance angles play in scoring goals is essential. In this section, we examine some ideas that affect scoring angles and your success as a goal scorer.

The High-Percentage Red Zone

Many coaches believe that the key area of the ice for scoring is the so-called red zone that extends from immediately in front of the goal area to the tops of both face-off circles (see figure 3.1). From this area, shooters have a greater possibility for scoring directly or off a tip-in or redirected pass. Estimates vary from level to level as to the exact percentage of goals originating from within the red zone. Statistics show that even at the pro levels, up to 80 percent or more of all goals scored originate from the red zone, making it a prime location for potential goal scorers to establish position.

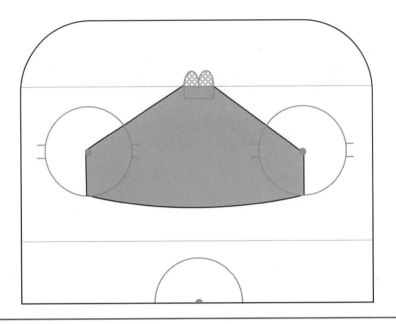

FIGURE 3.1 The red zone is the prime scoring area.

From a shooter's perspective, the appeal of the red zone makes perfect sense because the angle taken directly in front of a goalie gives more areas of the net to shoot for, as opposed to being off to either side, where the more acute angle diminishes the shooter's view of the net. This is often referred to as a "goalie's angle," which implies that the goaltender has an advantage. Getting into the red zone is akin to entering the key, or "the paint," in basketball. This is prime real estate for hockey players, and whoever controls that portion of the ice usually controls the outcome of the game. For shooters and goal scorers, getting into the red zone is a major objective of every game.

"Eyes" of the Puck

If we imagine that the puck could see where it was heading, would its perception of prime scoring angles and opportunities be the same as that of the player controlling the puck? Remember that players shoot either from the left or the right side; the puck is normally held from three to five feet away on either side rather than directly in front of the body. This means that shooters will see one perspective from their location, whereas the puck would have quite a different view (see figure 3.2).

Always keep in mind that puck location will affect your angle of attack for shooting, which in turn affects scoring opportunities and outcomes.

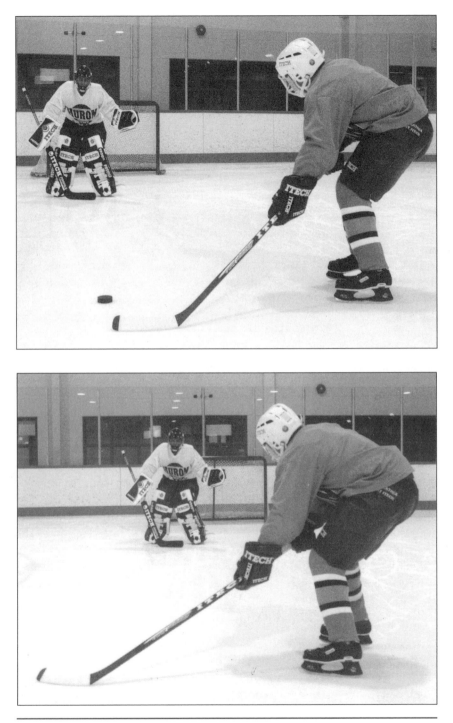

FIGURE 3.2 Puck eyes (top) versus shooter's eyes

Great scorers try to position the puck in an optimal scoring angle as opposed to the goalie's angle. They do this by putting the puck, not their body, as close to the middle areas of the red zone as possible given time and space constraints. You probably have heard coaches tell their players to "get to the middle of the ice" when approaching the red zone so that scoring chances are improved. What coaches should really say is, "Get the puck to the middle of the ice." The moral of this lesson— "Think like a puck before releasing the shot."

Aim for a Target Area

Very few players even at the professional levels can consistently hit a very small target area with a shot, especially when under pressure during a game and often at less-than-ideal angles to the net. Instead of shooting for openings just big enough for a puck to squeeze through, players should shoot at squares approximately one foot by one foot. Shooting at a larger opening provides some grace area in case your shot isn't perfect, and it rarely is. By shooting at bigger areas, a missed shot will often still be a shot on goal, whereas shooting too finely can result in the shot missing the net altogether. What you are doing is building in a margin of error when you give yourself more area to shoot for.

To drive this point home, try this activity in practice. Decide that one of the goal posts is going to be your target, not the open part of the net. If you take 10 shots and aim dead center on that goal post, you might be lucky to hit exactly in the middle of your target one time. In a game situation, that means that many of your potential scoring chances will fall wide of the net if you cut the target area too finely.

However, if you move that target over by only one foot toward the middle portion of the net, suddenly a shot off the mark can still find the mesh in the back of the net. In addition, depending on the angle at the point of contact between the puck and stick, a shot that misses the net can clear the zone around the corner boards, killing any potential offensive attack. The old saying "The perfect is the enemy of the good" applies to shooting and goal scoring. Don't try to be too perfect with every shot, and you will be surprised at how many imperfect shots look perfectly marvelous once they hit the back of the net!

Pressure the Defense

Players who are on the attack can generally enhance their scoring chances by pressuring both the defensemen and the goalie. When entering the offensive zone, players should be skating hard to the net (the red zone!), forcing defensemen to make split-second decisions to commit to your moves or to the puck. Fortunately, some of their decisions will be poor ones. By having players crowd the front of the net, you can effectively screen or distract the goaltender, adding increased pressure and confusion. A screen shot for goaltenders is a difficult direct shot to stop, and this situation might also lead to tipped or deflected shots for goals. Even if a goaltender has established perfect position and has an angle advantage over the shooter, a puck can still find the net if pressure is factored into the equation.

Use the Quiet Zone Behind the Net

Many goals start from the dangerous area directly behind the net and goaltender known as the quiet zone. Although the killing shot might occur in the red zone, many of the plays that lead to a goal start in this quiet zone where players are often out of sight and out of mind. Establishing puck possession in this area forces your opponents to look back or behind, which is both uncomfortable and disadvantageous, especially for the goaltender. While the goalie must turn his head to maintain eye contact with the puck, the attacking players have the luxury of always facing the puck and waiting for an outlet pass. Defenders must often turn their backs on dangerous opponents to front the puck and prevent someone from skating out from behind the net and scoring an easy goal.

Designing plays that originate in this quiet zone is an effective way of increasing goal-scoring opportunities. This area of the ice represents an excellent opportunity to confuse defenders, especially the goalie, and can result in a change of the angles held by opposing goaltenders, defensemen, and defensive forwards. From a shooter's perspective, anything that can disrupt proper defense is an offensive tool that must be used.

The drills in this chapter allow players to shoot from a variety of angles and positions. In many activities, the goalies will have the angle advantage; in other activities, shooters will be in the prime red zone or set up behind the net in the quiet zone. By trying these activities, players will begin to see where the greatest success is achieved in scoring goals. Don't simply be a passive participant in these activities, but instead, watch and learn from your practice so that game time will find you in prime scoring locations.

11 FULL RAPID FIRE

PURPOSE

- To practice accurate shooting on the net from the sideboard area
- To allow goalies to set proper angles for side shots

EQUIPMENT   None

TIME   3-4 minutes

PROCEDURE — Full-Ice Drill

1. Players are in one of two equal groups at either end of the rink and are positioned in opposite corners.
2. Coach blows the whistle, and three players from both ends skate in single file with a puck toward the opposite end of the rink as shown.
3. Players shoot the puck on net once they are positioned between the blue line and top of the face-off circle, allowing the goalie enough time to reset after each shot, then skate quickly to the other corner in the same end.
4. Once all players have shot, retrieved a puck, and assembled in the corner, the drill begins again with the next whistle.

KEY POINTS

- Players should push or drag the puck rather than overhandle it while moving up ice. This will reinforce the concept of breakaway speed and reduce unnecessary loss of control.
- Players should be looking up ice to identify goalie position. Remember as well to keep enough spacing between players so as not to hit the player in front with a shot.

DRILL PROGRESSIONS

- Increase speed component of the drill.
- Have players begin with backward skating, adding a turn or pivot near the red line area to practice skating and puck control skills.
- Add greater separation between players and have shooter go to the net as a screen and rebounder for the next player in line.

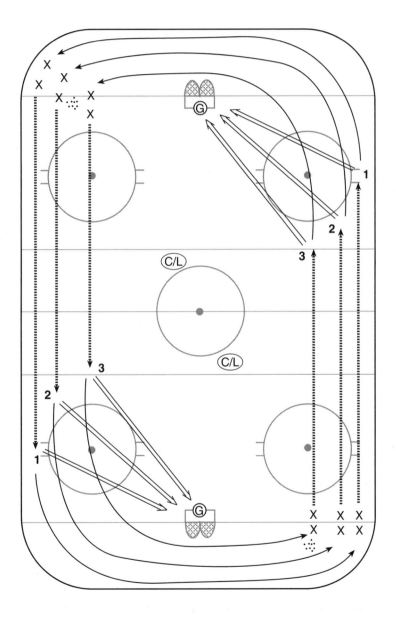

FULL-ICE ANGLES

PURPOSE

- To practice shooting from a variety of angles and distances
- To reinforce the notion of "breakaway speed" while controlling the puck through a pivot

EQUIPMENT   None

TIME   3-4 minutes

PROCEDURE — Full-Ice Drill

1. Players are in one of four lines at one end of the rink.
2. The first player in line one begins by skating backward until a pass is received from first player in line two, at which time they pivot and skate forward toward the opposite end. Player in line two begins the same sequence after releasing the pass to line one and the drill continues. Players in line one will eventually pass to line four.
3. Players should stay in their specific lanes to provide goalies with a variety of different angle shots, releasing the shot between the blue line and face-off circle.
4. Players remain at the end where they shot and assemble to begin drill in the opposite direction.

KEY POINTS

- Try different types of shots during each set.
- Players should remember to rotate their heads and shoulders earlier for quicker turns out of the pivot.
- Players might also consider executing a change of pace during their open ice skating at both blue lines and center red line as well.

DRILL PROGRESSIONS

- Add tight turns at each blue line to reinforce puck-controll skills.
- Send the second player in each line as a backchecker to add pressure to the drill.
- Have players do the entire drill while skating backward until they reach the far blue line.

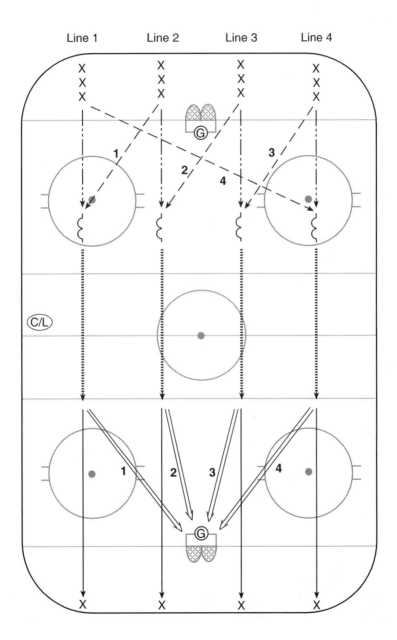

Line 1   Line 2   Line 3   Line 4

13 TEAM ROCKETS

PURPOSE

- To practice cutback moves through the neutral zone leading to a shot opportunity
- To focus attention on scoring angles, rebounds, and tip-in opportunities

EQUIPMENT   Four pylons

TIME   3-4 minutes

PROCEDURE — Full-Ice Drill

1. Pylons are near each blue line face-off dot in the neutral zone area.
2. Players are in one of four equal groups in each corner of the rink.
3. Coach blows whistle, and three players from each group A begin skating with pucks, following the route as diagramed. Players are approximately 10 feet apart.
4. All players cut around pylons as shown, and after shooting one at a time, they stop in front of the goalie and wait for the next player to shoot. Once completed, players stay in that end and opposite groups B begin on the next whistle.

KEY POINTS

- Players must stagger the start so that shooter has time to get to the front of the net for the next shot.
- Players should keep the feet moving throughout this drill; no gliding around pylons.
- This activity forces goalies to fight through screens to see the shot while reacting to rebound opportunities.

DRILL PROGRESSIONS

- Start the drill by having players begin with their knees on the ice, or lying on their back or stomach, forcing them to work on agility.
- Have skaters make tight turns around pylons.
- Use only one puck, which the three skaters must pass a designated number of times during the sequence.

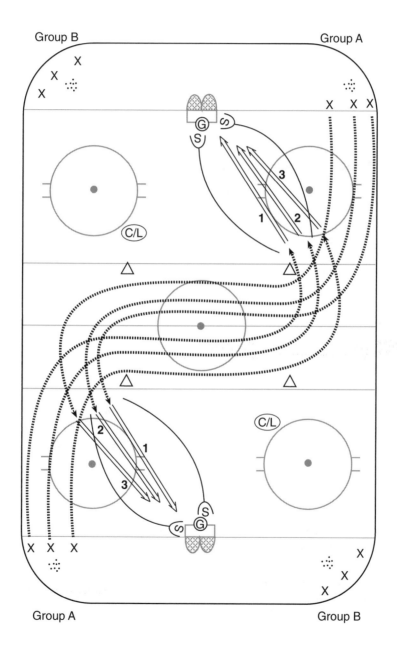

14 DOUBLE WING

PURPOSE

- To reinforce puck-control skills and shooting accuracy from different angles

EQUIPMENT   None

TIME   3-4 minutes

PROCEDURE — Half-Ice Drill

1. Players begin in a line along the red line in the center face-off circle with pucks.
2. First player skates along the center line to the far boards, then quickly turns up ice and receives a pass from the next player in line.
3. Attacking player then attempts to shoot as quickly as possible, follows shot to the net for a possible rebound, and returns to center by skating up the middle of the ice.
4. Player who passed the puck then skates across the center line in the opposite direction and drill continues with a pass from the next player in line.

KEY POINTS

- Players must turn to both their strong and weak sides in this drill.
- Focus is on quick feet and hands, with minimal backswing before shooting.
- Shooters should move quickly to the net for second-shot opportunities, then clear the zone as fast as possible.

DRILL PROGRESSIONS

- Shooter may begin by skating backward to the boards, then pivoting to forward skating while receiving a pass.
- Allow shooter to use escape move (a tight turn toward the boards) upon entering the zone, followed by a quick shot (see diagram).
- Use the passer as a late-arriving teammate who receives return pass before shooting.

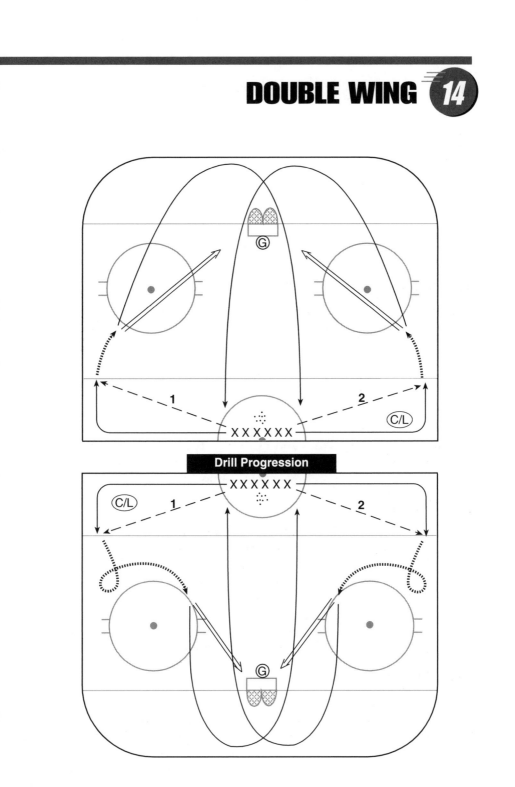

Drill Progression

15 AGAINST THE GRAIN

PURPOSE

- To provide practice in changing direction quickly in preparation for a shot opportunity

EQUIPMENT   None

TIME   3-4 minutes

PROCEDURE — Half-Ice Drill

1. A follow-up to Drill #14, with players assembled along the center red line in the center face-off circle.
2. First player skates along the center line and receives a pass from the next player in line.
3. Upon entering the offensive zone, the skater then cuts hard toward the middle of the ice and straight-line skates parallel to the blue line, releasing a shot and following it to the net.
4. Shooter then exits the zone along the sideboards from the same side as the play came from and returns to the line. The player who passed the puck initially then skates along the center line the other way, and the drill continues in the opposite direction.

KEY POINTS

- Players make two hard and powerful cuts in this activity and should attempt to keep their feet in motion while doing so.
- The concept of moving into the most dangerous scoring area, the red zone, is reinforced through this activity.
- Goaltenders should remain square to the shooter, using proper foot setup and angling technique. Squaring means that the shooter sees the biggest possible target in the goalie as he uses the leg pads, blocker, and catching glove to cover most of the net.

DRILL PROGRESSIONS

- Begin drill with backward skating and add a pivot.
- Have a coach in the corner who will feed a second puck to shooter once the initial shot is taken, forcing the shooter to attack the net (see diagram).
- Have initial shooter skate to the goal line before challenging next shooter.
- Alternate sides for the drill, and change position of coach for second pass.

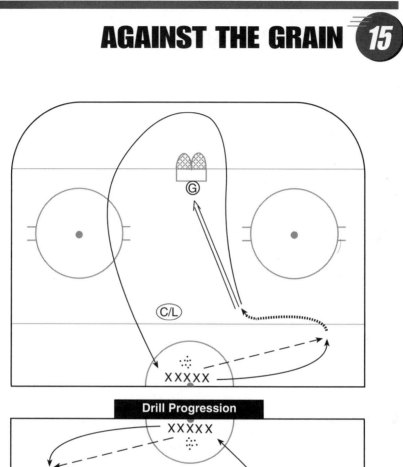

Drill Progression

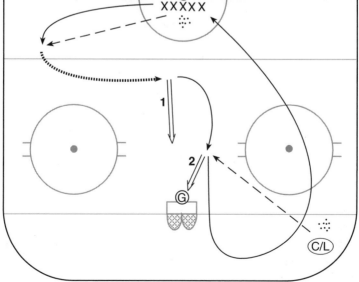

16 RAZER'S EDGE

PURPOSE

- To practice passing and receiving, puck control, and shooting from an angle

EQUIPMENT   1 pylon

TIME   2-3 minutes

PROCEDURE — Half-Ice Drill

1. Players are in one a group situated between the blue line and red line along the boards.
2. First player executes a tight turn and begins skating across the ice and receives a pass near the far boards from next player in line.
3. Puck carrier then cuts around pylon and sets up for a shot from the top of the face-off circle.
4. After shot is taken, the attacker follows for any rebound chances, then skates hard to the back of the line along the sideboards as drill continues.

KEY POINTS

- This is another activity that forces players to gain control of a puck and turn a transition opportunity into a shooting chance.
- As with most drills in which cutting is involved, players should attempt to keep their feet in motion.
- Goalies are focusing on proper setup for one side only, allowing no short-side goals.

DRILL PROGRESSIONS

- This can become a corner drill with shooter taking the puck to the goal line near the corner and attempting to beat the goalie in tight (see diagram).
- Passer can be used as a passing or rebound option at the net by entering the play from the other side of the ice.
- Have first shooter finish by stopping in front of the goalie and setting a screen for the next shooter in line.
- Try the drill from the opposite side of the rink so players can practice shooting from both angles.

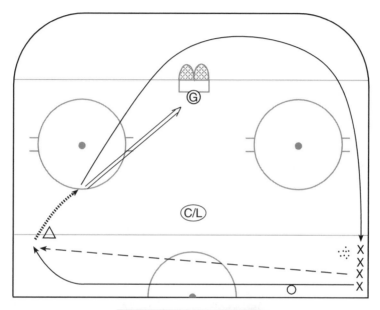

Drill Progression

RAZER'S EDGE II

PURPOSE

- To reinforce skating and puck-control skills, leading to shot opportunities from many angles
- To practice goalie positioning for corner shots

EQUIPMENT 2 pylons

TIME 2-3 minutes

PROCEDURE — Half-Ice Drill

1. A follow-up to Drill #16 with players assembled near the sideboards in a group between the red and blue lines.
2. First player skates forward, then initiates a pivot and skates backward toward other side of the rink.
3. Next player in line passes a puck that the first skater receives near the far boards, followed by another pivot to forward skating. The skater goes past the two pylons before shooting.
4. Original passer then becomes the next shooter, and the drilling continues.

KEY POINTS

- This should be done at high tempo, which will force players to handle the puck under difficult turning conditions.
- Shooter may either shoot from the extreme angle or cut toward the net and try to hit an opening from close range.
- Goalies must deny any short-side opportunities.

DRILL PROGRESSIONS

- Give shooter the option of going to the back of the net for a wraparound shot from either direction (see diagram).
- Have passer skate into zone with a second puck with the initial shooter acting as a screen, also attempting to deflect the second long-range shot.
- Remember to try this drill from the opposite side of the rink to practice shooting from both sides.

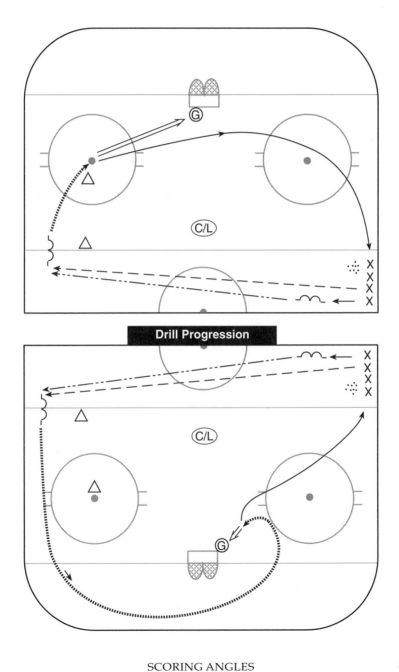

Drill Progression

18 NEWT'S DELAY

PURPOSE

- To work on puck control, passing, and timing to set up a shooting and scoring chance

EQUIPMENT   2 pylons

TIME   3-4 minutes

PROCEDURE — Half-Ice Drill

1. An additional follow-up to Drills #16 and #17 with players along the side boards in a group between the blue and red lines.
2. First player begins with a puck and makes a tight turn before skating around the pylon on the opposite side of the rink.
3. Puck carrier heads to the corner and executes an escape move (turn) along the sideboards.
4. As the first player is completing the escape move, a second player in line skates around the closest pylon and moves toward the front of the net for a pass from puck carrier who goes quickly to the net for any rebound opportunities.

KEY POINTS

- Timing is important for the second player, who should not leave too quickly to join the attack.
- Puck carrier must have eyes on the passing targets as soon as possible to ensure an accurate pass.
- Second player should call for the puck when entering the scoring area.

DRILL PROGRESSIONS

- Have two players enter the zone as possible shot options by skating around the near pylon, with the puck carrier making the decision as to which player will receive the pass (see diagram).
- Have puck carrier go to the back of the net as a safety zone and pass from either side to the second player who follows, forcing goalie to be alert.

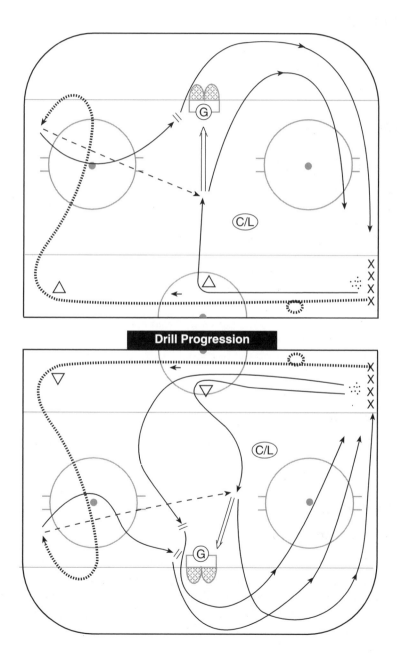

Drill Progression

NEWT'S DOUBLE 'D'

PURPOSE

- To improve puck-control turns and timing while setting up for a shot opportunity

EQUIPMENT   3 pylons

TIME   2-3 minutes each side

PROCEDURE — Half-Ice Drill

1. Set up pylons on the ice as shown.
2. Follow up Drill #18 with players along the sideboards in a group between the red and blue lines.
3. First player begins drill by executing a tight turn with puck, then skating around the far pylon to the corner of the rink where an escape move (turn) is completed.
4. As first player completes the escape move, a second player follows by skating around the middle pylon, where she receives pass from first player and also executes an escape move.
5. Third player cuts around closest pylon as soon as the previous second player executes the escape move and receives a pass from this player, finishing the drill with a shot. All three players then return to their group.

KEY POINTS

- Timing is a key component of this drill, and players must be patient.
- The first and second skaters should drive to the net after passing the puck, stop near the side of the net, and look for any rebound opportunities.

DRILL PROGRESSIONS

- Allow the last player with the puck a variety of options, including passing to one of the other two players for a redirected shot or tip-in play, or moving directly behind the net to set up a passing opportunity (see diagram). Escape moves can be made optional.
- Add one or two defensive players who defend against the first two skaters in the drill.

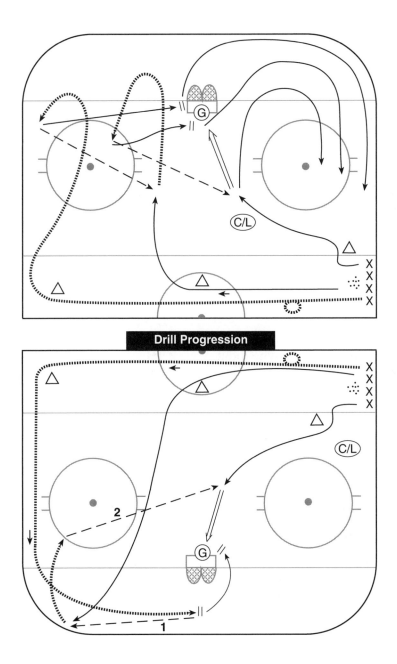

Drill Progression

20 EMPTY TANK

PURPOSE

- To force players to concentrate on shooting on-target from a distance
- To provide an enjoyable conditioning activity

EQUIPMENT   None

TIME   5-7 minutes

PROCEDURE — Full-Ice Drill

1. Players are in one of two equal groups at either end of the rink and are positioned in opposite corners at or near the hash marks.
2. On the whistle, three players from each group skate with pucks behind the net, making sure that they do not skate beyond the goal line.
3. All players attempt to shoot the puck into the empty net at the other end of the rink.
4. If one or more of the three scores, no conditioning skate occurs. If all three miss the target, the entire group of players in that end, including those who did not shoot, must do two complete laps of the ice. The drill then continues with the next group of three players after any necessary laps have been completed.

KEY POINTS

- This is a fun activity that players will enjoy.
- Hitting the open net is more difficult than players think, so conditioning will occur.
- Try this activity from both sides, switching location halfway through the activity.

DRILL PROGRESSIONS

- For an interesting progression, players should try this using their backhand.
- For goalie conditioning, have goaltenders sprint from the bench area once shooters are rounding the net and attempt to stop pucks from entering the net.

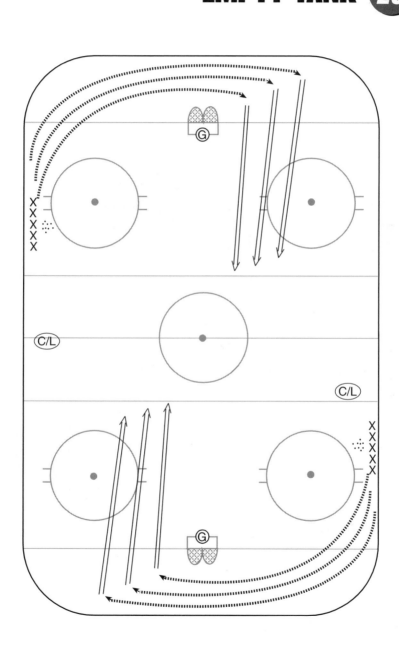

4 Scoring Games

In virtually all sports, effective offensive play occurs when players have great confidence in their abilities. Often we hear of athletes who are "in the zone" or at a "comfort level" that permits them to perform with tremendous success. A key to performing at this level is the ability to concentrate or focus fully on the changing situations of the game. In his best-selling book *Successful Coaching,* coach and author Rainer Martens refers to this as the "flow experience" and describes athletes as being "so intensely centered on the activity that concentration is automatic."

How can hockey players more consistently move to these states of precision and refined execution in scoring? Part of the answer is that players must be allowed to get into their so-called comfort level through drilling activities, and coaches can play a major role in this regard. Instead of relying on the same practice day after day, which often acts to stifle creativity and offensive development, coaches should include drills and games that are fast paced and interesting, drills that allow players to work on offensive skills such as scoring. The fun environment generated by games helps advance the feeling of getting into a rhythm of shooting and scoring, which is part of this idea of being in the zone.

Sometimes a game may be included simply for the sake of playing and having fun as a team, perhaps an activity that is completely different from anything normally done on the ice. For example, a 5-on-5 football game on the ice in the middle of a practice that is not going well can suddenly bring new life to the players. The same idea can be modified into a 5-on-3 football game in which contact is not allowed and the emphasis is on passing lanes and scoring goals (touchdowns). Use your imagination and intuition when deciding on the types of games your players might enjoy and benefit from.

Scoring and Face-off Games

Scoring and face-off games are often overlooked yet vitally important parts of team preparation that coaches and players should remember to practice. During the course of any hockey game, each team will have a limited number of opportunities to face off in its opponent's end of the rink. Each one of these situations could result in a good shot on net that can often lead to a direct or rebound goal. Considering the number of goals scored in an average game, face-off preparation becomes more important. Some coaches are including face-off work as a function of bigger practice activities, whether in the form of minigames, special teams play, or individualized competitions. Make the time to reinforce and practice proper face-off technique and include different face-off plays that your team uses as a part of your scoring games. Players will soon come to realize how key this aspect of play can be in the offensive part of the game.

The drills in this chapter are predominantly minigames within the bigger game of hockey that will foster creative offensive play. These activities should be mixed in with other drilling patterns from time to time because players will benefit skillwise while being invigorated for the remainder of practice.

FIVE-PUCK FINISH

PURPOSE

- To practice goal-scoring technique through a fun activity

EQUIPMENT   None

TIME   5-7 minutes

PROCEDURE — Half-Ice Drill

1. Three forwards are positioned in the offensive zone along with a defenseman positioned at the blue line. Five pucks are placed at different locations in the zone as well.
2. When the coach's whistle blows, a designated forward controls one of the five pucks and may shoot or pass to any of the other forwards or the defenseman. The objective is to score by any means possible.
3. Once a goal is scored or the goalie smothers a puck, another attack occurs with another of the five pucks. Drill continues until all five pucks have been played.
4. Shooters decide among themselves when each will shoot so as to avoid having multiple shots taken at the same time.

KEY POINTS

- This activity is tough on goalies and should be discussed before the drill begins.
- Players should attempt to make accurate passes that result in quality scoring chances, and everyone should be poised for any rebound chances.

DRILL PROGRESSIONS

- Add one defensive player to keep the attackers moving and thinking about open lanes.
- Force players to make at least one pass to the defenseman with each puck (see diagram).
- Insist on one screen shot from the defenseman during each five-puck segment.

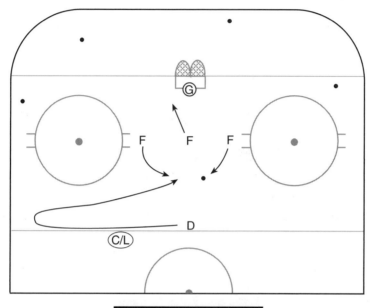

Drill Progression

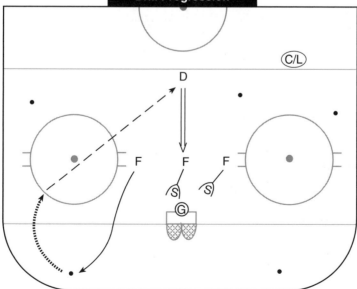

22 HEADS UP

PURPOSE

- To practice puck control with the eyes focused ahead, not down, in preparation for shooting
- To condition the players

EQUIPMENT   None

TIME   4-5 minutes

PROCEDURE — Half-Ice Drill

1. Players begin by stickhandling a puck in a stationary position just inside the blue line.
2. Coach is positioned near the net. Players must maintain eye contact with the coach during the stickhandling sequence.
3. Whenever the coach nods his or her head or points a stick at a specific player, the player skates forward and engages the goalie with a shot or deke.
4. After shooting, the player skates to the goal line, pivots to backward skating below the face-off circle, then pivots forward again at the hash marks before completing a sprint to the center red line.
5. The player then returns to the original shooting line.

KEY POINTS

- Players must keep focused on the coach, and if they miss their notice to shoot, then a suitable "punishment" is levied by the coach.
- This is a high-activity drill with shooters coming forward every 2 to 3 seconds.
- Goalies must pick up movement in front of them quickly to make a save.

DRILL PROGRESSIONS

- Have players shoot long shots with coach passing a second puck for an in-close scoring chance (see diagram).
- Coach might call for a specific shot or shot location (e.g., "top left, wrist shot")
- Allow dekeing the goalie.

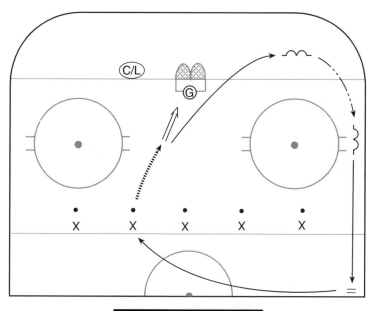

Drill Progression

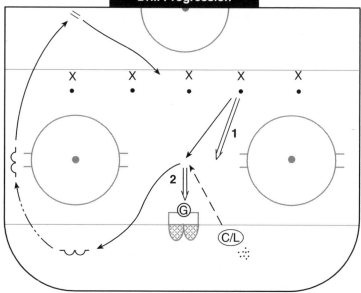

23 LADDER GAME

PURPOSE

- To practice puck possession and finding openings for scoring

EQUIPMENT   None

TIME   4-5 minutes

PROCEDURE — Full-Ice Drill

1. Players begin in two equal groups on opposing benches with one player from each bench entering each zone as a puck is put first into one corner then another by a coach (two games are going at once, one in each end zone).
2. Two defensemen are positioned at each blue line and support whichever player gains possession of the puck, setting up a 3-on-1 situation with the remaining player from the bench.
3. Whenever a goal is scored, another puck is dumped into each zone by the coach. One additional player from each team enters the play to a maximum of five for any one group (making it a 5-on-3), including the two defensemen.
4. Coaches will put a new puck in the corner whenever a goal is scored, the puck leaves the zone, or the goalie controls it. New players enter on coach's whistle.

KEY POINTS

- Players should be reminded that new participants enter both ends when the whistle is blown and can position themselves on the bench for easy entry onto the ice, depending on which end they are going to.
- Players should use the defensemen to create more time, space, and goal-scoring chances.
- Keeping score is an option that can also be used.

DRILL PROGRESSIONS

- Create outnumbered situations by restricting players from one team to enter the play, which will increase offensive opportunities.
- On a long whistle, the players switch ends, meaning that games move from one end of the ice to the other end at top speed (keep the eyes up during this transition!).

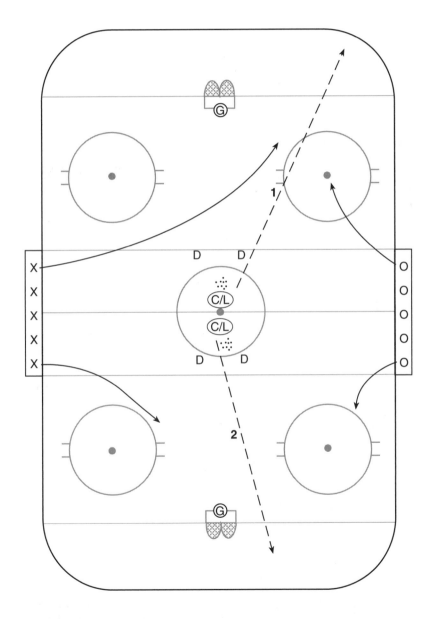

24 SURVIVAL

PURPOSE

- To maintain puck control under pressure while creating shooting and scoring chances
- To condition the players

EQUIPMENT   None

TIME   10 minutes

PROCEDURE — Full-Ice Drill

1. Players are in two equal groups and seated at one of the two bench areas.
2. The coach has pucks that are shot in succession into different areas of the ice on the whistle.
3. The first players in line on the respective benches jump over the boards and play 1-on-1 with their opposite from the other bench.
4. Players can score on either net, and the coach can have as many 1-on-1 situations in play as he or she wishes. However, neither player can leave the ice until one of the two players scores a goal.
5. With each new puck put into play, players next in line on either bench jump into the action.

KEY POINTS

- This is an exhausting drill that is fun, yet it is a real test of skill and conditioning.
- If three nets and goalies are available, use them. Skaters can go to any net to score a goal, often changing direction in the neutral zone and going to the opposite end to escape the defender.
- Players should be told that goals will only be counted if they are shot along the ice when shooting from longer distances. This will help ensure the safety of the goalie in case of multiple shots at the same time.

DRILL PROGRESSIONS

- Make it a 2-on-2 activity using the same rules of play.
- Have players keep count of their total goal output during the drill, with the highest total receiving some form of reward for their efforts.

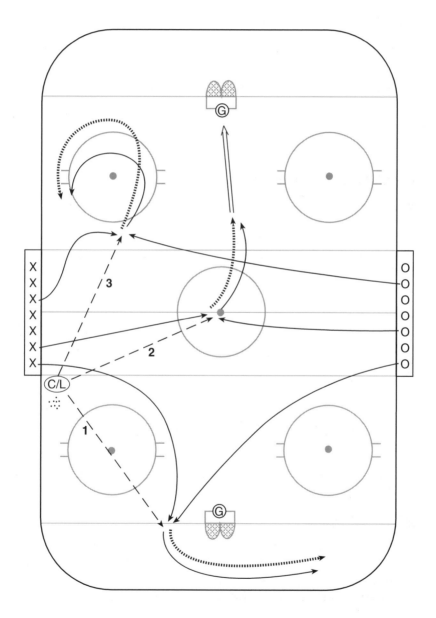

COACHES' CHOICE

PURPOSE

- To provide a variety of situations in which players can improve puck-control and shooting skills

EQUIPMENT   None

TIME   10 minutes

- Includes time for shift changes, no more than 30 seconds

PROCEDURE — Full-Ice Drill

1. Players are divided into two equal teams, one on each player bench.
2. A designated player or coach for each team will call out a number from one to five on the whistle, and a corresponding number of players will enter the ice surface. Any number combination is allowed, meaning that teams could be in a 5-on-1 situation, 3-on-2, 2-on-4, etc.
3. Play continues until the next whistle, when a new combination of players jumps over the boards and enters the play.
4. A number can only be used once, resulting in a total of five shifts during a given sequence.

KEY POINTS

- Opposing teams and designated number caller should not know what the other team is calling. Numbers are called only when the whistle blows, resulting in a fun activity with a variety of circumstances.
- Players will begin to discuss strategy to be used dependent on their situation, whether at an advantage or disadvantage.

DRILL PROGRESSIONS

- Add a second puck to the activity to "overload" the drill.
- Allow teams to pull their goalie if so desired to gain an extra attacker.
- Contact can be made optional.

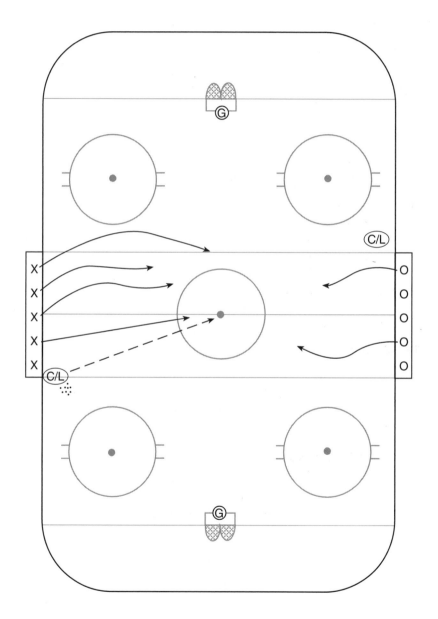

26 WILD CARD 3-ON-3

PURPOSE

- To practice offensive skills, including shooting, through a fun activity

EQUIPMENT   None

TIME   5 minutes

- With a whistle and change every 20 seconds

PROCEDURE — Full-Ice Drill

1. Players are divided into two equal teams on player benches.
2. Whistle is blown, coach puts a puck in play, and three players from each bench jump onto the ice and compete 3-on-3 full ice until the whistle blows to signify a shift change.
3. Coaches are wild cards who can take any loose pucks and pass to any open player.
4. All three players must touch the puck before a shot can be taken.
5. If a goal is scored, a coach will put another puck into play.

KEY POINTS

- This is a tremendous activity that makes players aware of open lanes and that forces defenders to lock on coverages.
- Coaches might designate a particular shot to be used during a specific sequence.

DRILL PROGRESSIONS

- Include a three-stride rule in which players must pass before skating beyond a three-stride range.
- One-time shooting can be made the rule for goal scoring with only this type of shot counted as a goal.
- Contact can be optional.

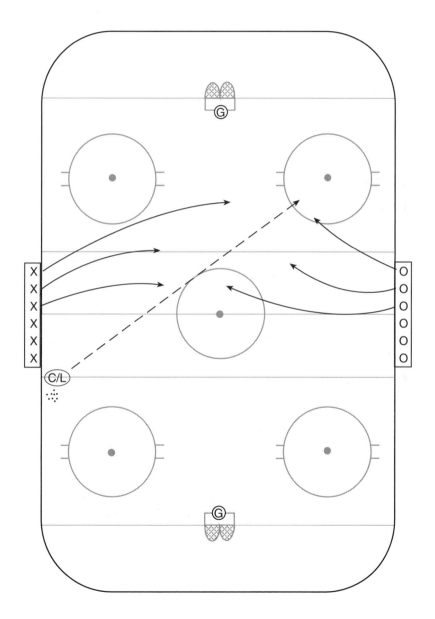

SAFE HOUSE 3-ON-3

PURPOSE

- To simulate a game situation in the offensive corner leading to a shot on goal

EQUIPMENT   None

TIME   5-7 minutes

- With a whistle and player change every 30 seconds

PROCEDURE — Half-Ice Drill

1. Players are arranged in two teams in the neutral zone.
2. One player for each team is in the "safe house," an area in either corner of the rink, and goals are placed widthwise across the ice near the hash marks in either face-off circle.
3. On the coach's whistle, two players from each team enter the zone and play a 3-on-3 that includes the safe house players. The corner players cannot be attacked and must touch the puck before their team can score a goal. They cannot move out of the corners.
4. Play continues until the next whistle, when two new players enter. Rotate the safe house players every third shift.

KEY POINTS

- Players must get in a position to receive the pass very quickly after they release the puck to the corner players.
- Players should call for the puck and break for openings.

DRILL PROGRESSIONS

- Attempt "one-time" passes, where the puck does not stop but is always being "bumped" from teammate to teammate.
- Use boards, where applicable, instead of passing directly.
- Use the coach as another player for your team (see diagram).

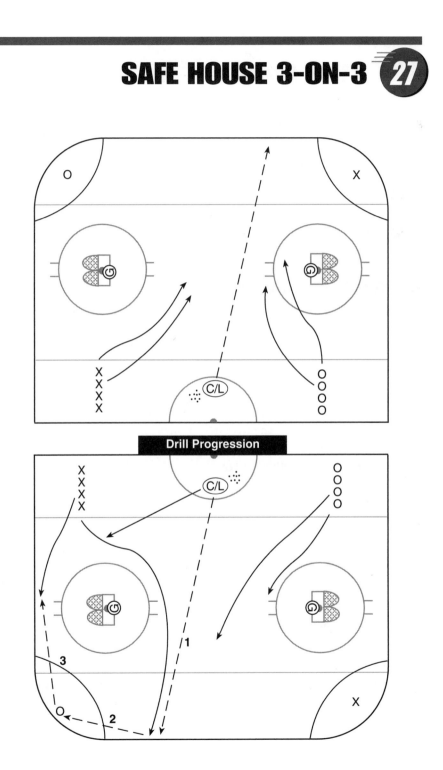

Drill Progression

28 BUZZ SAW

PURPOSE

- To practice passing give-and-go by identifying open teammates, resulting in a shot on goal

EQUIPMENT   None

TIME   5-7 minutes

- With a whistle and player change every 30 seconds

PROCEDURE — Half-Ice Drill

1. Similar situation to Drill #27, with two teams set up in the neutral zone and one player in the corner for either team.
2. On the coach's whistle, three players attack for one team, two players from the other as designated by the coach, making the drill a 4-on-3 (including corner players). The coach puts all pucks in play.
3. When coach yells "go" approximately 10 seconds later, a defenseman positioned at the blue line joins the team that is outnumbered, making the drill a 4-on-4.
4. The designated team that incorporates the defenseman must use that player for any shot on goal. The defenseman has the option to shoot or pass during this drill but must skate along the blue line only and cannot move into the attack zone.

KEY POINTS

- This is an excellent drill for making forwards aware of the importance of defensemen in offensive attacks.
- The defenseman should focus on not having shots blocked while shooting from the blue line.

DRILL PROGRESSIONS

- Allow defensemen to penetrate the middle portion of the zone for shooting opportunities.
- Add a second defenseman to create a temporary 5-on-4 situation (see diagram).

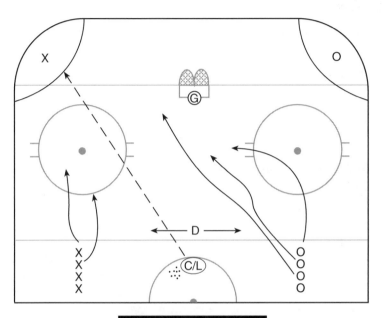

Drill Progression

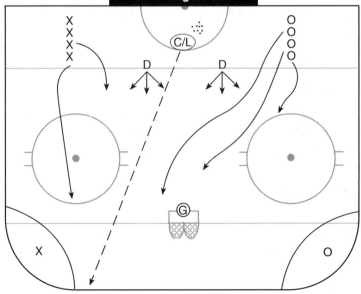

29 SPECIAL TEAMS RALLY

PURPOSE

- To create a controlled environment in which players attempt to set up for a goal-scoring shot

EQUIPMENT   None

TIME   10-12 minutes

- With a whistle and player change every 60 seconds

PROCEDURE — Full-Ice Drill

1. Players are in one of two teams situated along the boards on either side of the ice between the red and blue lines.
2. One team is designated power player for five consecutive shifts while the other team penalty kills.
3. On the whistle, the power-play team sends five players into their defensive zone to receive a puck from the goalie and begins the offensive attack. Penalty killers set up between the red line and their defensive blue line and cannot advance beyond the center red line for the purposes of this drill.
4. Play continues until a goal is scored, the puck is smothered by the goalie, or the defenders clear the puck beyond the blue line.
5. When play is finished, next attack begins with new players for each team. Once five rushes are completed, teams switch roles.

KEY POINTS

- This is a fun activity in which puck control is a key element of creating the best shooting opportunity.
- Keep score to see which team does the best job of working the power play.

DRILL PROGRESSIONS

- Add pressure by adding a designated backchecker who skates from the far end when instructed by the coach, restricting setup time for the power-player unit and turning the drill into a 5-on-5.
- Start with a basic penalty-kill system, then add different variations.
- Have defenders play with sticks turned upside down.

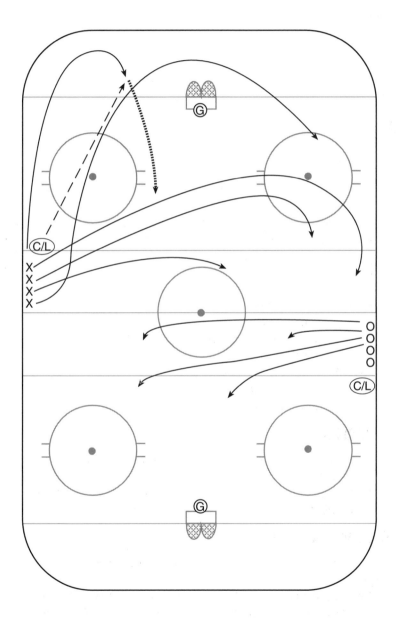

⟨30⟩ COLORADO SPECIALS

PURPOSE

- To use puck control in a power-play situation leading to a goal-scoring opportunity

EQUIPMENT   None

TIME   8-10 minutes

PROCEDURE — Full-Ice Drill

1. Split team into two groups, and alternate the drill within the two end zones.
2. One group of five players (power play) stands on the blue line and waits for the coach to put a puck in the corner. A group of four penalty killers is 10 feet behind the group of five in the neutral zone between the blue and red lines and enters the zone second. This will allow the power play to gain possession of the puck and set up (top half of diagram).
3. Play continues with passing and shots on goal until a whistle is blown and another puck is put into the other end of the rink. Five new players are waiting to attack, and the previous power-play personnel (minus one player who is told to drop off) skate hard to the opposite end and become the penalty-killing unit.
4. This sequence continues with each succeeding whistle.

KEY POINTS

- The coach will designate one power-play person to drop off on the ensuing rush.
- This is a nonstop, fun activity that allows players to try both power-play and penalty-killing assignments.

DRILL PROGRESSIONS

- Have two players drop out and make the next series a 5-on-3 power play.
- Practice 6-on-3 by pulling the goalie on some occasions.
- Restrict contact by defenders, which will allow skill development and a "comfort zone" for offensive players.

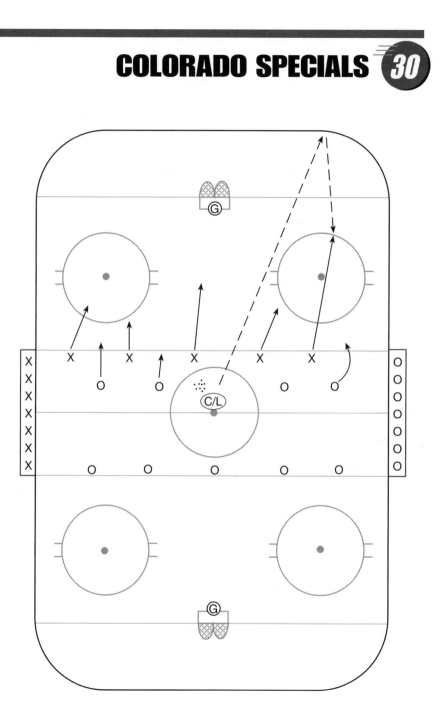

© Casey B. Gibson

Scoring Under Pressure

From 20 feet in front of a goaltender, a puck shot at 50 miles per hour enters the net in less than one second. With so little time to react, you can understand why goalies have difficulty making saves on shots from close distances. If the shot is accurate, a goal is even more likely to be scored. So, if it's so easy, why don't players score more often?

One of the reasons is pressure. It might be easy for some players to skate in alone on a goaltender during practice and release a booming shot into the upper corner of the net while the goalie lunges in vain. But put that same player under attack during a game situation when pressure is a variable, and the same outcome isn't so easily achieved! Football coaching legend Lou Holtz tells the story of a field-goal kicker who once told his coach that "I'm a good kicker; I just have trouble kicking when you're lookin'!" To which Holtz replied, "Well, son, I plan on being at most of the games, so we have a problem!"

Players must become accustomed to pressures, both mental and physical, because these are intrinsic to most sports. Players can do this by constantly visualizing pressure situations during practice, perhaps even by playing mental games in which the next shot wins it in overtime. Coaches can help by ensuring that players are served a regular helping of pressure activities during every practice session.

This concept of pressure can be applied in different ways during any team practice. We often think of a 1-on-1 confrontation as the ultimate pressure situation, yet this can come on the ice in many shapes and forms. Indeed, having a defender confronting you on a consistent basis through drilling activities might be the best game simulation available. In many situations, this kind of pressure can be applied by using a trailing checker—a player who constantly nips at the heels of the puck carrier.

Other methods reinforce this concept as well. For example, restricting the amount of space used in drills forces players to react more quickly while developing skills that allow for immediate escape from a defender. A drill might also be modified to include time constraints. When time becomes a factor, such as reducing the time allowed for a shot, players must respond to pressure with quicker decision making.

Developing Pressure Skills

Although an on-ice activity might not necessarily be a contact or pressure drill by design, pressure could in many cases be added. As you read and come to know the drills in this book, try to visualize how an activity might be adapted to the use of pressure by adding physical contact, time restrictions, or space constraints. By doing this, you can bring your practices closer to game play. Here are some simple yet effective tips for players and coaches to consider for developing prime-time players who perform when the heat is on.

Try to Buy Time

"Buying time" is best illustrated by the escape move, in which a player makes a very tight turn or pivot to evade a defender. Perhaps the greatest player ever at using this technique is Wayne Gretzky. Here is a player of average height and weight who consistently outplays opponents who have greater speed, size, and strength. As you watch him play, you'll notice that during key moments when he is working his way into an opponent's end, he often makes a sudden turn or cutback move to evade a defender. This move buys time, which allows teammates to join the attack and make the situation more dangerous for Gretzky and his colleagues.

You don't always have to be in control of the puck to use this skill. Often, teams that employ a tight checking system will have players away from the puck closely watched and covered as well. This situation demands awareness and an ability to get out of this kind of pressure. By using an escape move, with or without the puck, you put yourself in a better position to buy extra time during pressure situations, which inevitably translates into better decision making during a hockey game.

Maintain Control of the Puck

Learning how to use your feet to control the puck when you are being pressured is a great advantage in hockey, something that many European players possess because of their training as soccer players. 1-on-1 confrontations, especially along the end- and sideboards, become more challenging as you move higher and higher in to the hockey ranks, so learning how to handle this pressure and maintaining puck possession become increasingly important. Players soon realize when holding a puck in their feet along the boards that their bodies can be effectively used as a shield against pressure, in which the arms and rest of the upper body hold off the attacker while the legs, feet, and rest of the lower body control the puck. Having the skill, strength, and patience to control the boards, what players often refer to as "the wall" or "the rail," is truly a plus in handling overall game pressure.

Use Picks and Screens

We often hear the terms "pick" and "screen" associated with basketball, such as when a player receives a pass off a "pick and roll" or "back-door screen." Hockey teams employ the same kind of blocking tactics as well, although any player attempting to screen for a teammate must clearly establish position.

For example, a player holding his or her territory in front of an opponent's net engages a defender, which provides a passing lane for a teammate who is close by. If the offensive player in front of the net has position, he does not have to move to take a pass. To stop a potential shot on goal, the defender has to take the long way around.

Focus on Technique

Focusing on technique is a valuable tip for any player in any sport because virtually every sporting contest has some form of pressure, be it physical, mental, or a combination of both. For example, many professional golfers will tell you that when the heat is on with a money putt on the line, they do not think about the outcome of the stroke; instead, they concentrate on making a solid technical putt. Can you imagine standing over a ball and saying to yourself, "This putt is worth one hundred thousand dollars, and if I don't make it, I'll look like a fool!" Chances are you *will* end up looking like a fool because your focus is not on the actual shot, it's on the outcome. The same is true in hockey when players often focus on things such as the amount of time remaining in the game, the size of their opponents, or other factors that take away from concentrating on more important things. Learning to focus on proper execution will assist greatly in reducing the effects of pressure, and this ability is something that can be achieved through constant reinforcement and practice.

The drills assembled for this section force you to shoot and score goals under great pressure and stress. Most of the drills are helpful in reinforcing second effort, especially after that first shot has been saved and the second shot could produce a goal. By constantly exposing players to these kinds of drilling situations, the pressure becomes less of a distraction and more of a basic aspect of play. Eventually, with enough exposure to pressure scenarios, many players will learn to react instinctively.

31 ROBERTSON'S ROAST

PURPOSE

- To introduce basic shooting activities in which pressure is included

EQUIPMENT   None

TIME   2-3 minutes

PROCEDURE — Half-Ice Drill

1. Players begin in pairs, with one player at the top of the face-off circle and the other on the goal line.
2. The player on the goal line passes a puck to his partner, who cannot move until the pass is received. The passer then moves up and stops at the face-off dot.
3. After receiving the pass, the player with the puck must skate from the goal line toward the partner and cannot release a shot on goal until within a stick length of the partner, whose job is to make contact with the shooter.
4. Both players go to the net for any rebounds and battle for puck possession. The players then switch roles for the next turn.

KEY POINTS

- The player about to be hit cannot shoot from long range but must carry the puck into "traffic" and find a space to shoot through.
- Defending players should not reach for the puck with their stick but make contact to simulate a game situation in close to the goalie.

DRILL PROGRESSIONS

- Have a second puck behind the net that both players attempt to control after the first shot (see diagram).
- Start the drill with players on their knees or lying on their stomach to encourage quickness.

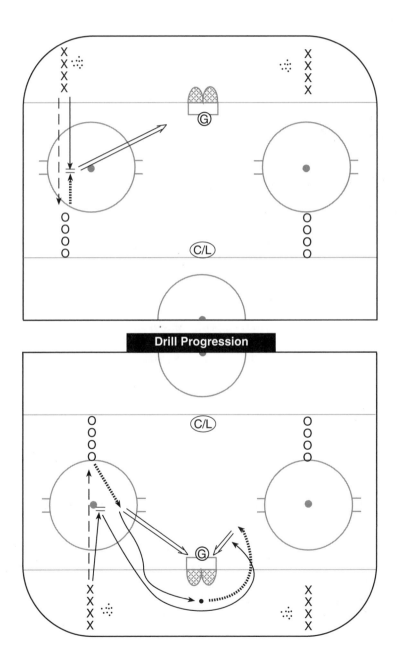

Drill Progression

# GREASE

PURPOSE

- To practice evading defenders in the goal area to create scoring opportunities

EQUIPMENT   None

TIME   5 minutes

- 15-20 seconds per engagement

PROCEDURE — Half-Ice Drill

1. Players begin in pairs directly in front of the goalie with one partner, the attacker, using a stick, and the other player, the defender, using only her shoulders, arms, and hands.
2. The attacker attempts to create open space in front of the goalie by evading the coverage of the defender and continually looks toward the corner where an additional player (or coach) is waiting to pass the puck.
3. Passes are made from the corner player until the whistle is blown, with the attacker looking for clear shots, tip-ins, and redirects.
4. Additional pairs of players are near the coach and enter the play when so instructed.

KEY POINTS

- Players stay in a small area of ice directly in front of the goalie with little skating required.
- The attacker should keep his stick close to the ice for quick tips and one-time shots.

DRILL PROGRESSIONS

- Have both players use sticks.
- Put players in groups of three with one attacker and two defenders. This forces attacker to rotate from one opponent to the other and look for scoring areas to penetrate.
- Add another passer, rotate sides from which the pass originates (see diagram).

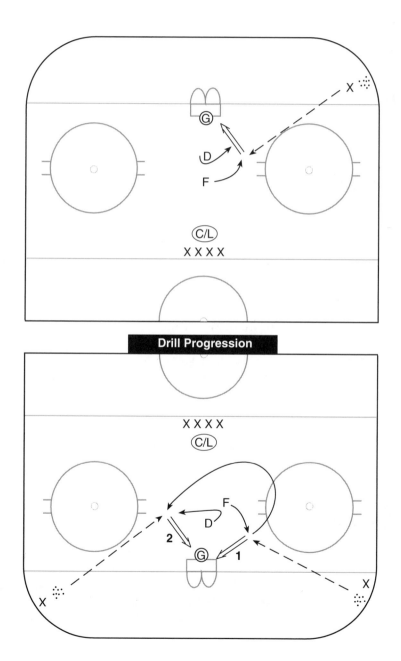

Drill Progression

33 GREASE FIRE

PURPOSE

- To create offensive situations that simulate game conditions, leading to scoring chances

EQUIPMENT   None

TIME   5 minutes

- 15-20 seconds per engagement

PROCEDURE — Half-Ice Drill

1. This drill is similar to the previous drill (Drill #32) with some variation. An attacking defenseman is added at the blue line, and a forward is also added, making the drill a more offensive threat than the previous version.
2. The attacking defenseman has puck and begins the play either by passing a puck to the player who is stationary in the corner or by shooting directly on net. This attacking defenseman may move along the blue line only and is not allowed to advance into the zone.
3. The two forwards in front of the net look for quick passes and redirects from either the defenseman or the corner passer.
4. If a goal is scored, the attacking defenseman puts another puck in play.

KEY POINTS

- It is important that the two forwards work to get open dependent on the puck location.
- Forwards should move into areas where deflections can be attempted and rebounds jumped on.

DRILL PROGRESSIONS

- Have corner passer move to the back of the net for different attack positions.
- Have attacking forwards attempt to "pick" the defenseman, and screen for the shooter (see diagram).

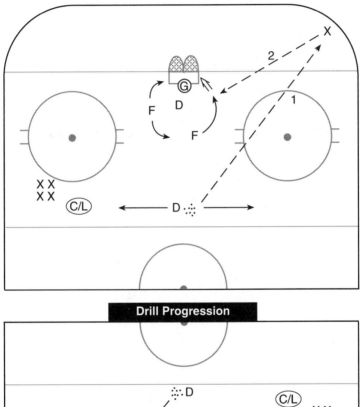

Drill Progression

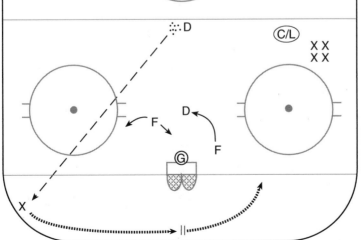

34 GRUNT DRILL

PURPOSE

- To practice shooting off the wing while under pressure
- To condition the athletes

EQUIPMENT   None

TIME   5-7 minutes

PROCEDURE — Full-Ice Drill

1. A player from the designated shooting line at either end of the rink is positioned at the hash marks while a player from the defending line is positioned at the bottom of the face-off circle.
2. On the whistle, the shooter sprints forward and receives a pass from the coach in the center ice area. The defender also leaves on the whistle in pursuit of the shooter.
3. The defender chases the shooter the length of the ice and attempts to prevent a shot on goal.
4. Players go to the back of the lines in the end where the shot is taken and switch roles.

KEY POINTS

- Player with puck maintains control, with second effort a key to success, especially after the shot when looking for rebounds.
- The defending player tries to stop any shot from occurring. If the first shot is taken, defender works to restrict any second-shot opportunities.

DRILL PROGRESSIONS

- Add a second defender positioned at the far blue line to assist the first defender as the play heads to the net.
- Force the attacker to stay wide by putting pylons deep into the corner, which will allow the defender additional time to cut off the attack.

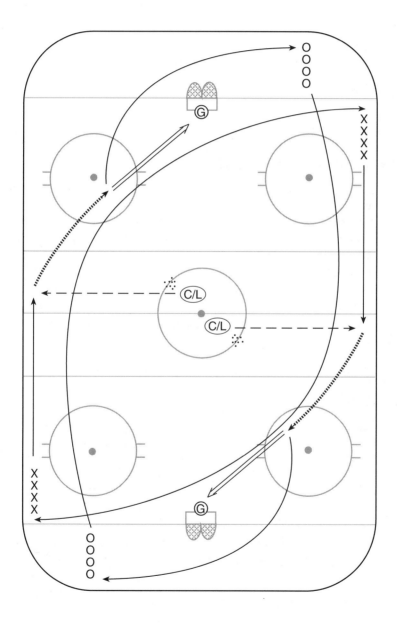

 **BACK DRAFT**

PURPOSE

- To improve passing and receiving with pressure as a means of achieving a quality scoring chance

EQUIPMENT   None

TIME   3-5 minutes

PROCEDURE — Full-Ice Drill

1. Players are split into four equal groups, one each positioned in the corners of the rink.
2. Two players, one from each group at the same end of the rink, mount a 2-on-0 attack, making sure to pass at least twice during their trip down the ice before shooting on goal.
3. As the shot is taken, two players from the opposite groups begin a similar 2-on-0 attack, going in the opposite direction from the first group. The two players who started the drill become defenders after shooting and pursue the second pair in a backchecking fashion.
4. Once any pair has shot at one end and backchecked toward the other, it goes back in line and waits for its next turn.

KEY POINTS

- This is a fast-paced, continuous drill that provides pressure from behind, forcing attacking players to make quick shooting decisions.
- Defenders attempt to check by using the stick or body. But they do not finish their checks because the attackers must be allowed to regroup for their checking roles immediately after their attack.

DRILL PROGRESSIONS

- Add a defenseman, creating a 2-on-1 attack that provides pressure from the back and front.

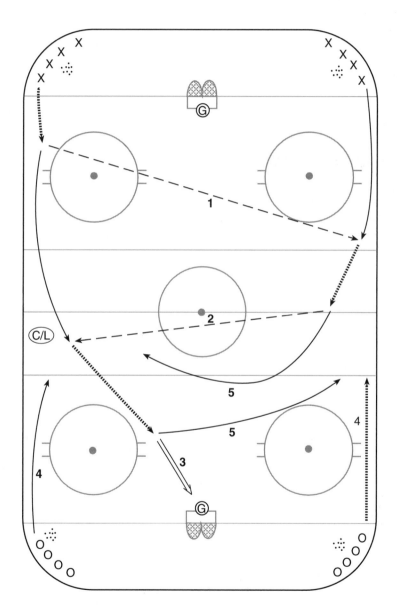

36 THE VISE

PURPOSE

- To reinforce quick hands and feet during a pressure scoring situation

EQUIPMENT   4 pylons

TIME   2-3 minutes

PROCEDURE — Half-Ice Drill

1. Players are paired and split into two even groups in each corner of the rink, two lines per group.
2. On the whistle, a puck carrier from one side only must go between the pylons positioned at the blue lines before he is "live," at which time the defender can attack. The puck carrier attempts to fake the defender and get to the net quickly for a scoring chance.
3. The defender cannot go beyond the blue line and must wait for the puck carrier to pass through the pylons before attempting to defend the attacker.
4. Once play is completed, the players return to their corner, and the other corner groups begin.
5. Once both groups have completed one round of the drill, players switch roles, and the drill begins again.

KEY POINTS

- The puck carrier needs to work at using effective shoulder and head fakes to gain an advantage on the defender.
- This is a great second-effort drill that is a good conditioner as well.

DRILL PROGRESSIONS

- Have attacking player begin without a puck, skate through the pylons, and receive a pass from the next player in line (see diagram).
- Add a second defender in front of the net who restricts shooter from getting rebounds, forcing a second effort to score.

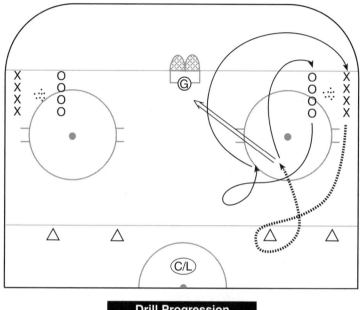

Drill Progression

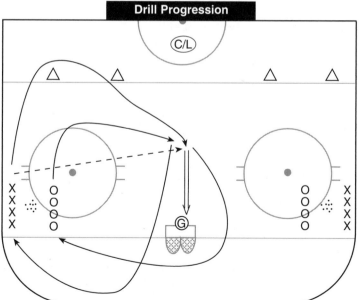

37) CIRCLE WAR

PURPOSE

- To increase conditioning and practice controlling the puck using a wraparound shot under pressure

EQUIPMENT   4 pylons

TIME   5-7 minutes

PROCEDURE — Full-Ice Drill

1. Players are in four equal groups tight to the boards in each corner of the rink, with the two groups designated *A* always going at the same time. The two *B* groups go together as well.
2. Coach blows the whistle, and one attacking player at either end picks up a puck, skates around the nearest face-off circle, and shoots on net.
3. After completing the shot, the attacker retrieves another puck near the hash marks along the boards and begins to skate at top speed around the center face-off circle, moving toward the other face-off circle in the zone. As the second puck is touched by the shooter, a second player pursues the puck carrier around the entire course, attempting to dislodge the puck.
4. Puck carrier skates around the net for a wraparound shot.
5. Players then skate back to their original lines and switch roles.

KEY POINTS

- Puck carrier must keep feet moving throughout the drill, while the defender tries to strip the puck and eliminate the puck carrier.
- This drill reinforces puck-control skills at high speed, leading to a seldom-practiced scoring chance, the wraparound.
- Goaltender must be alert as play comes behind the net.

DRILL PROGRESSIONS

- Allow the puck carrier the option of cutting in front rather than behind the net, which will restrict goalies from "cheating."
- Have another puck available that a coach or player at either end puts into play once the wraparound attempt is finished, adding a second-effort component to the drill.

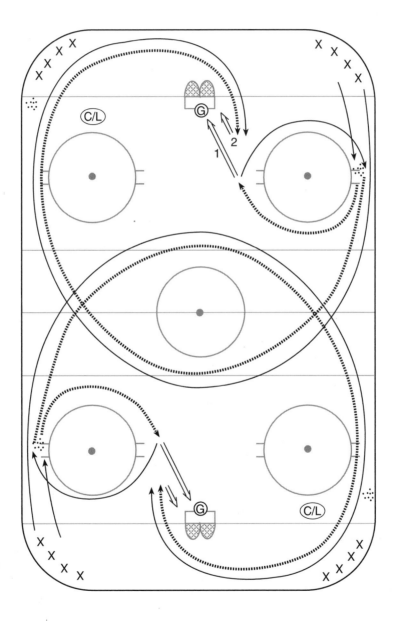

ON FIRE

PURPOSE

- To practice puck control at high speed and under pressure, leading to a scoring opportunity

EQUIPMENT   2 pylons

TIME   5 minutes

PROCEDURE — Full-Ice Drill

1. Players are in four equal groups, each above one of the hash marks along the boards in each corner of the rink. Players are facing the near endboards (goal line). All the defensemen are in the center circle waiting their turns. When lying on the ice at the blue line, they should be facing in the direction from which their opponent is coming.
2. On the whistle, a player from opposite diagonal ends begin with a puck, skating full speed behind the goal and faking a player from the opposite line, who is waiting on the face-off dot in the opposite circle.
3. Once this initial defender is evaded, the defenseman waiting at the blue line jumps up and skates backward around the pylon at the center face-off circle and plays a 1-on-1 with the attacker. The play is finished with an attempted shot on goal.
4. The next two players in the opposite two groups leave when the next whistle is blown.

KEY POINTS

- This drill encourages attackers to stay wide and use acceleration as a means of getting good shooting opportunities.

DRILL PROGRESSIONS

- Add a backchecker from the start of the drill to increase pressure.
- Have attacker play a second puck out of the corner once first shot is taken.

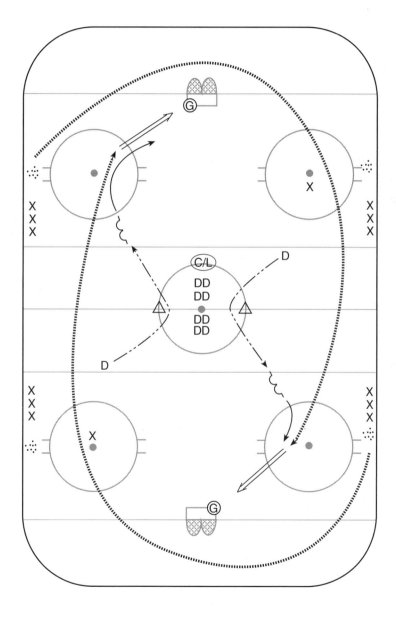

SHUT DOWN

PURPOSE

- To practice full-ice competition for puck control in a 3-on-3 drill

EQUIPMENT   None

TIME   4-5 minutes

- 20 seconds maximum per group

PROCEDURE — Full-Ice Drill

1. Players are in two equal groups along opposite boards in the neutral zone area.
2. Coach places puck in a corner, and two players from each team enter the playing area with one team gaining possession, the other team defending.
3. Whichever team gains puck possession first has a third attacker who joins in immediately, giving that group the advantage (3-on-2) for a brief time, approximately 3 seconds. On the whistle, the other team has a third player enter the play, making it a 3-on-3 drill. The team with the 3-second advantage must quickly read where the open teammate is and connect with a quick pass.
4. Play is finished once the shot is taken, and new players begin.

KEY POINTS

- This drill has a time pressure attached to it, which forces the controlling team to make a quick decision on offense.
- The third person entering the play must look for openings and avoid being contained or pressured, all the while calling for the puck.

DRILL PROGRESSIONS

- Limit the time pressure even further.
- Have each group of players design its own "automatic" plays with everyone attempting the same play, such as lead passes off the sideboards only, cycling behind the net, etc.

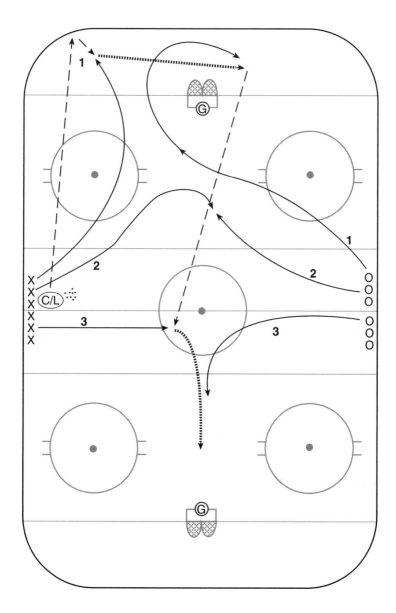

BEAT THE BOX

PURPOSE

- To practice focusing on shooting and scoring under extreme pressure in front of the net

EQUIPMENT   None

TIME   3-4 minutes

PROCEDURE — Half-Ice Drill

1. One player will be the shooter with four defenders who form a box or square around the shooter in front of the net.
2. Pucks are with a designated passer in each corner; one of the passers will attempt to pass the puck whenever the shooter calls for it.
3. The shooter rotates in and out of the box but may call for a pass only when inside the box, with defenders attempting to force the player by making stick or body contact.
4. Shots can only be taken when the shooter is inside the box.

KEY POINTS

- Passing players must wait for the shooter to call before passing, which reinforces communication between players.
- Shooter has the option of which passer to call.
- Whichever defender the shooter is skating toward while moving through the box is allowed to meet the shooter and make contact. Defenders will not do a lot of skating but will instead hold their position.

DRILL PROGRESSIONS

- Force shooter to stay within the box for the last 10 seconds of the drill.
- Add another attacker in front of the net who acts as a screen and goes for any rebounds (see diagram).

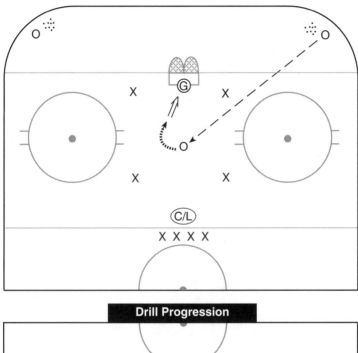

Drill Progression

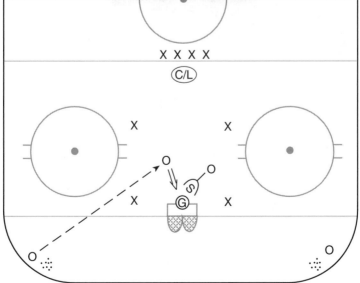

6 One-Time Shooting

It has been argued by many sports enthusiasts that hitting a baseball is among the most difficult of all sporting skills to master. Add to that list of difficult skills "one-time shooting." One-time shooting refers to an attacking player shooting a puck immediately off a pass from a teammate, often while skating at high speed. This skill requires great concentration because you must be able to find the puck which often arrives through a congested area immediately in front of the opponent's net.

As players gain maturity and continue their ascent up hockey's developmental ladder, they find that one-time shooting is one skill that often separates the contenders from the pretenders! Many elite coaches will watch carefully to see whether players can consistently deliver on this skill before allowing them to move into higher levels of play.

Developing One-Time Shooting Skills

To successfully shoot a puck off the pass while in motion, you should consider the following important concepts: focusing on the puck until it is released from your stick, seeking optimum position away from the puck, and getting the shot off.

Focus on the Puck

Most great athletes, irrespective of the sport, are able to focus or concentrate on the immediate task at hand. They have an ability to block out other aspects of play to achieve something very specific at a particular moment. In one-time shooting, this could mean watching the puck as it moves through a maze of legs, fighting off a defender, trying to get your stick flat on the ice surface, positioning for the shot, and releasing the shot before the defense can react. Focus is a key mental element for virtually all aspects of hockey, none more so than shooting to score off a pass.

Seek Optimum Positioning

As mentioned in chapter 1, optimum positioning is an often overlooked yet important aspect of offensive production. Players must learn to position themselves where they can most comfortably receive a pass to release quickly. As a general rule, this means that the potential shooter's body should be open, or facing the direction from which the puck is coming, with knees bent and weight distributed to protect against defensive pressure. Also, the stick should be low to the ice and in the ready position, much in the way that as a tennis player brings the racket back in preparation for making contact with a tennis ball. By having the stick in this position, fewer misfires will occur, and the one-time shooter will save valuable split seconds in stick preparation before the puck arrives.

In addition to setting their body position relative to the puck, players need to be searching for the best locations on the ice to shoot from. As any offensive play unfolds, players without the puck must become increasingly aware of "soft spots" or quiet areas in the defense where they can enter quickly and capitalize on a one-time shot, such as the area to the side of the goaltender away from the puck carrier. Players must learn to read proper angles of attack when heading for rebounds, remembering that few rebounds go directly to the area immediately in front of the goalie. Most rebounds will come out on an angle, and time and experience allow players to read where to be positioned in relation to where the shot comes from. Professional athletes such as Dino Cicarelli, Mario Lemieux, or Joe Sakic typify the kind of players who possess this ability to get open and then, most importantly, finish their scoring chances.

Get the Shot Off—On-Target

Have you ever heard it said that a basketball player has "a shooter's roll"? This saying implies that the shot was hardly a perfect one, but because of the player's great offensive skills, the ball somehow found the hoop. So too is there a shooter's roll in hockey. Often a player will attempt a quick release or one-time shot, mis-hit the puck, and then watch as it somehow trickles past a sprawling goalie as the red light is turned on. This is why it is important to get any shot on-target, perfect or otherwise, because every shot is a potential goal. The old saying that you score 0% of the shots you never take should be ingrained in every player's mind.

To better your chances of getting the shooter's roll with the puck, remember to use proper mechanics, staying bent at the knees so that you get more power for the shot. Also, sliding the bottom hand even lower on the stick shaft than normal and keeping the wrists tight will further help the shot make it to the target area. Although it might be true that "close only counts in horseshoes," sometimes being close with a one-time shot can be good enough to find the back of the net.

FLYER PEPPER

PURPOSE

- To practice quick release of shots in goal-scoring situations

EQUIPMENT   None

TIME   2-3 minutes

PROCEDURE — Half-Ice Drill

1. Players are evenly distributed at the hash marks in the end face-off circles and are facing the goal line. Two players are designated as passers and are halfway between the net and the boards along the goal line.
2. A player from one of the lines passes to the closest designated passer, skates toward the net, receives a return pass from the passer, and takes a one-time shot on the net. Once the shot is completed, the shooter skates to the back of the opposite line.
3. As the shot is finished, a player from the opposite line begins in the same fashion, and the drill continues alternating sides in this fashion.

KEY POINTS

- Shooters should concentrate on making a good first pass before proceeding to the net.
- Passers should make the return pass one that the shooter can re-lease immediately, meaning that the pass should be accurate, not too fast, and located right at the stick blade.

DRILL PROGRESSIONS

- Have shooters pass and skate around the top of the circle instead of cutting straight across to the net (see diagram).
- Include the opposite line as a rebound line so that two players head for the net at the same time (see diagram).
- Give passer pucks and have a second-shot option for the shooters.

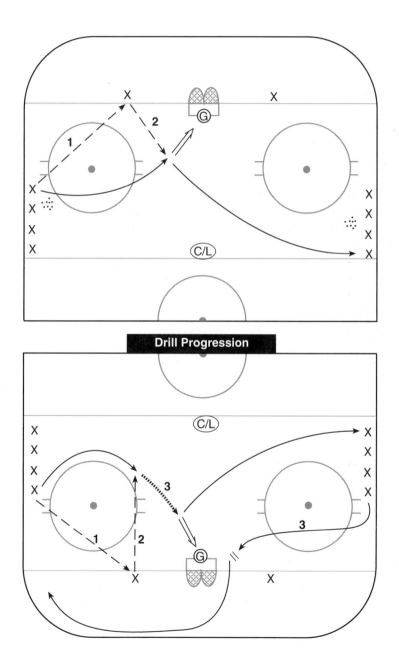

Drill Progression

ONE-TIME SHOOTING 123

THREE-SHOT PANIC

PURPOSE

- To practice shooting pucks in rapid succession using a one-time motion

EQUIPMENT   None

TIME   4-5 minutes

PROCEDURE — Half-Ice Drill

1. Split players into equal groups located in each corner.
2. Alternate sides with one player taking three shots consecutively, followed by a player from the opposite line.
3. First player skates around the face-off circle, receives a pass from the second player in line, and shoots on net. Player then skates around opposite face-off circle, pivots to always face the passer from the goal line in the opposite corner, receives a second pass, and takes a one-time shot on net. Player then skates around the first circle again, receives another pass from the same line, and finishes his third shot.
4. Player then goes to the back of the opposite line and another player begins.

KEY POINTS

- The shooter must always face the corner from which the next pass is coming, pivoting and skating backward where necessary.
- Players in groups waiting to shoot must be alert because the next player in line is a passer before becoming a shooter.
- Goalies must be conscious of angle changes during this drill to set up effectively for saves.

DRILL PROGRESSIONS

- Attempt the entire drill while skating backward, turning to face the passer only at the last moment before shooting.
- Add a tipper and rebounder to make the drill more difficult for goalies (see diagram).

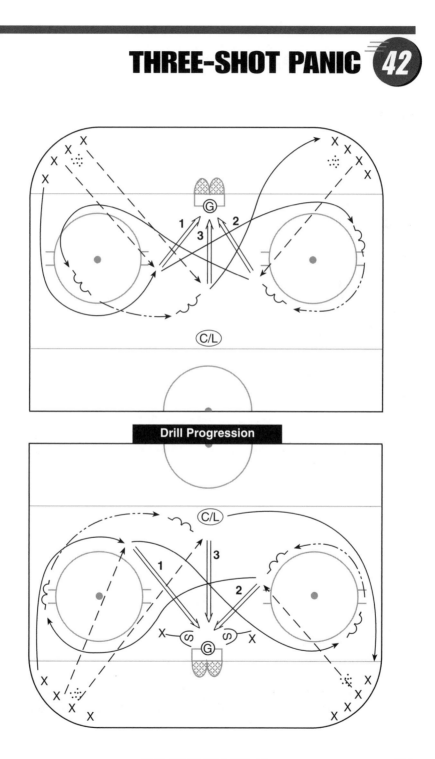

Drill Progression

JACKAL 2-ON-2

PURPOSE

- To practice puck control and shooting at high speed in a competitive situation

EQUIPMENT   None

TIME   3-4 minutes

PROCEDURE — Full-Ice Drill

1. Split players into two equal groups and have one group along either sideboard in the neutral zone area.
2. On the whistle, players at both ends begin by passing a puck behind their respective net, where the goalie sets it up for the player who made the pass.
3. As the player who initially passed the puck skates behind the net to retrieve it, a second player skates parallel to the blue line, waiting for a pass from the first player. A one-time shot must be taken as the pass is received, and the coach follows this by blowing the whistle.
4. As the whistle is blown, all four players on the ice skate toward the center face-off circle where an additional puck has been placed by the coach. The pair of players first to the puck attempts to score on the same end where it was initially shooting, while the other pair crosses the red line and attempts to defend.

KEY POINTS

- This is a competitive drill that is also a good conditioner.
- Emphasis should be that one-time shots are the priority, so this should be a fast-paced activity.

DRILL PROGRESSIONS

- Have a multiple-shot sequence in the respective ends before moving toward the center circle, with pucks available throughout the goal area to be retrieved by the passer.
- Add a third player for the second part of the drill as a designated shooter, someone who will come late into the attacking zone and call for the puck, making this a 3-on-2 finishing drill.

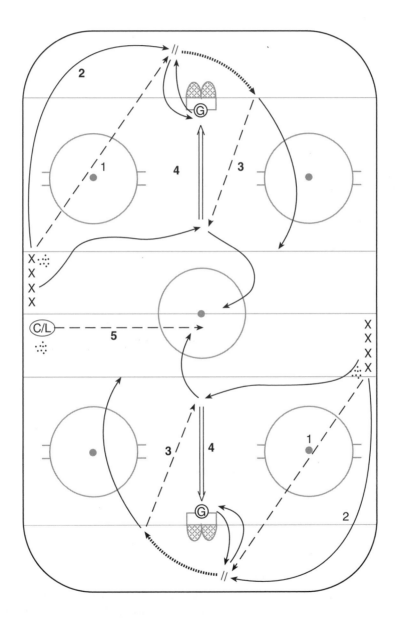

44 BACK-DOOR QUARTERBACK

PURPOSE

• To reinforce the concept of offensive attack from behind the net.

EQUIPMENT   None

TIME   4-5 minutes

PROCEDURE — Half-Ice Drill

1. Defensemen are positioned at the blue lines along the boards in two groups with forwards divided equally into three groups—two located by the board-side hash marks in each corner and one group positioned in the center face-off circle area.
2. Player skates with a puck from one of the groups of board-side forwards and is positioned behind the net while forwards from the other two groups skate to open areas in front of the net.
3. When the coach blows a whistle a player from one of the two defensive groups straight-line skates across the blue line, delaying so as to see which side the puck carrier will move toward.
4. Puck carrier has the option of passing to any one of the three players, who in turn initiate a one-time shot on the net. When the play is finished, the drill continues with a new set of players.

KEY POINTS

• Players must skate into areas where the puck carrier can make an easy pass.
• Passer should ensure that the goalie cannot deflect any passes by extending the goalie stick. Do this by moving far enough away from the net before passing to ensure an open lane.
• Potential shooters should attempt to position their body so as to get maximum speed on the one-time shot.

DRILL PROGRESSIONS

• Add a defender to force attackers to move into openings.
• Have two defensemen play their positions with multiple passes from behind the net, forcing the forwards to react quickly and get into the best position possible to tip or redirect a shot from the defensemen, who are ready also for any rebound chances (see diagram).

BACK-DOOR QUARTERBACK 44

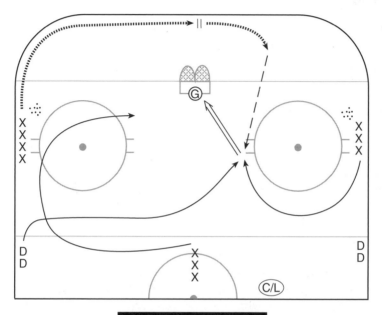

Drill Progression

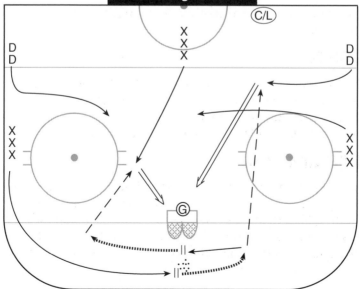

45 QUIET ZONE I

PURPOSE

- To promote puck-control skills through passing in the area directly behind the net for offensive opportunities

EQUIPMENT   None

TIME   4-5 minutes

PROCEDURE — Half-Ice Drill

1. Players are in one of two lines inside the blue line, with the coach positioned between the two with a supply of pucks.
2. Coach directs a puck into either corner, and two players attack, one from each line.
3. The player who retrieves the puck skates away from the net and passes the puck off the end boards in the opposite direction such that it lands on the far side of the goal.
4. The other player retrieves the puck and begins skating toward the end face-off circle while the first player turns and skates to the front of the net.
5. A pass is made, and a one-time shot is put on net; players return to their lines.

KEY POINTS

- Player who is shooting the puck should attempt to be at an optimal scoring angle near the front of the goal when receiving the pass, as opposed to staying at a wide angle.
- This is a timing play that takes time to perfect.

DRILL PROGRESSIONS

- Try this drill with an entire offensive line of three players with one designated as the high player who stays up near the blue line, adding both depth and another shooting option to the attack.
- Use a defender positioned between the hash marks who will have the option of attacking either player (see diagram).

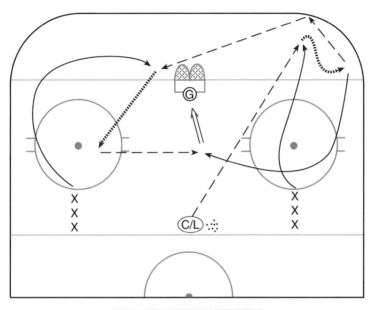

Drill Progression

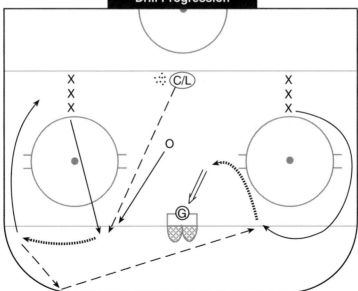

CURL RETURNS

PURPOSE

- To practice passing and neutral-zone regrouping as lead-ins for a one-time shot opportunity

EQUIPMENT   2 pylons

TIME   4-6 minutes

PROCEDURE — Half-Ice Drill

1. Team is divided into two equal groups with one group in a corner and the other group between the opposite blue line and red line.
2. The first player in the group at the blue line begins the drill by passing across the ice to the first player in the corner line, then receives a return pass near the face-off circle in the corner. Puck carrier must skate around the first pylon as positioned in diagram, returns a pass to the next player positioned in the blue line group, then skates around the second pylon.
3. The final pass is to the skater as he or she enters the offensive zone and positions the body for a one-time shot.

KEY POINTS

- Players should attempt to skate as quickly as possible throughout the drill without any gliding during turns.
- Passes should be one-time passes where possible.
- Change sides and positions of pylons after 2-3 minutes.

DRILL PROGRESSIONS

- Use a trailing checker who is constantly on the puck carrier's heels (see diagram).
- Position a coach in the corner for a second pass and shot opportunity (see diagram).

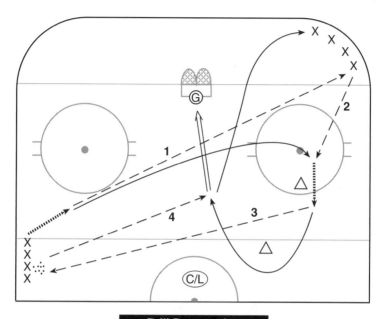

Drill Progression

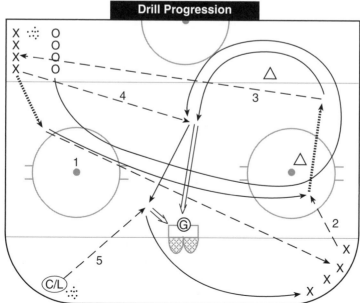

ONE-TIME SHOOTING   **133**

TWO-PLAYER DASH

PURPOSE

- To develop skating and timing during one-time shooting chances
- To include a conditioning factor in practice

EQUIPMENT   6 pylons

TIME   4-5 minutes

PROCEDURE — Full-Ice Drill

1. Split team in half with groups on either side of the center red line along one sideboard.
2. On coach's whistle, one player from each group skates the route as diagramed with only one player retrieving a puck at the blue line.
3. After skating behind the net at the other end of the rink, the player without the puck approaches the other end and times an attack on the net. The puck carrier delivers a perfect one-time setup pass.
4. Once the puck carrier releases the pass, he or she skates to the side of the net for any rebound chances. Alternate ends where puck is carried and shot.

KEY POINTS

- This drill makes for a high-speed and fun activity that forces players to look at each other and identify proper timing parameters.
- Puck carriers should be forced to pass backhand if that is the position of the puck as they exit the last pylon turn.

DRILL PROGRESSIONS

- Have players skate part of the course backward.
- Have each player carry a puck and use both a long shot and a one-time shot.

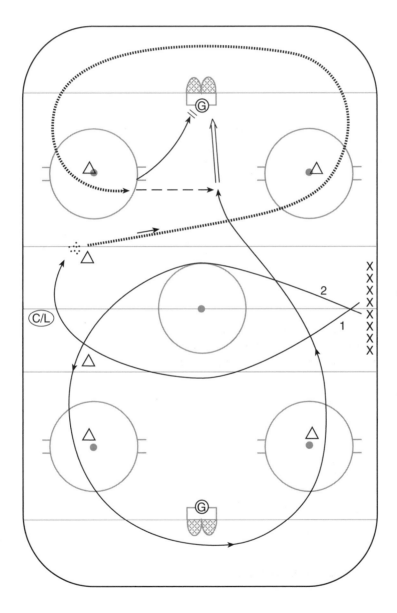

48 TRAPSHOOTING

PURPOSE

- To practice one-time shooting from a variety of angles in the offensive zone

EQUIPMENT   None

TIME   3-4 minutes

PROCEDURE — Half-Ice Drill

1. Players are in a group positioned outside the blue line.
2. Coach is along the near sideboard area with a supply of pucks and acts as passer throughout the drill.
3. First player begins to skate along the blue line and yells "Pull" whenever he wants a pass for shooting a one-timer.
4. A minimum of three passes are made from the coach during the sequence, with the shooter finishing the drill with a skating activity as diagramed.

KEY POINTS

- Players should attempt to control and then release the puck as quickly as possible because quickness of release is often more important to scoring than the actual speed of the shot.
- Focus on getting each shot on-target as a primary objective.

DRILL PROGRESSIONS

- Put a time limit on each shooter by which the entire drill must be completed.
- Have the skater move away from the passer for three shots, then skate back toward the passer for another three shots to complete the drill.
- Have players skate backward the entire route before shooting and complete the skating sequence at the end of the drill controlling a puck (see diagram).

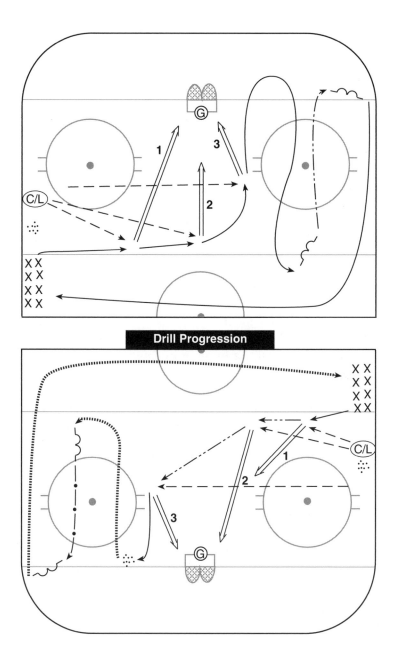

Drill Progression

ASSASSIN

PURPOSE

- To develop quick feet and hands in preparation for a one-time shot

EQUIPMENT   5 pylons

TIME   5-7 minutes

PROCEDURE — Half-Ice Drill

1. A variation of Drill #48. Players are in two equal groups in two corners. Two passers are positioned anywhere along the goal line as well.
2. A player from one corner begins the sequence by skating to any of the five pylons that are randomly placed within the zone. As the skater approaches the first pylon, one of the passers will feed a soft pass for a one-time shot.
3. The player must move to each of the five pylons and position for a one-time shot at each, never knowing until the last second which side the pass will come from.
4. Once the five shots are taken, a player from the opposite corner begins, and the drill continues nonstop.

KEY POINTS

- Passers can decide on a sequence of passing (alternate or otherwise) and vary the sequence for succeeding shooters.
- This is a very difficult drill that will force players to achieve proper body positioning given restricted time and space.

DRILL PROGRESSIONS

- Have player follow each shot for any rebounds, thus adding a conditioning element.
- Add defensemen to challenge each shot as it is taken, forcing the shooter to concentrate (see diagram).

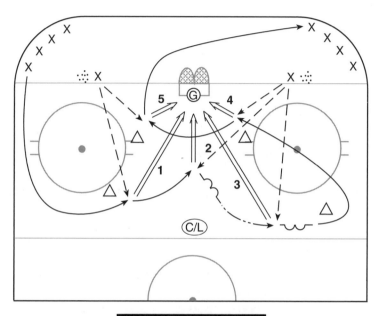

Drill Progression

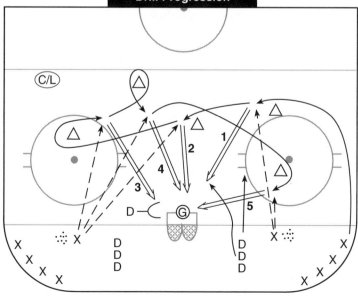

MERRY-GO-ROUND

PURPOSE

- To practice one-time passing as a lead-in to the one-time shot at high tempo

EQUIPMENT   None

TIME   3-5 minutes

PROCEDURE — Full-Ice Drill

1. Team is in four equal groups at the blue line areas along either board with a passer positioned along the goal line in every corner of the rink.
2. One player from group *A* and another from group *B* start, on the coach's whistle, by skating to the far side of the center face-off circle with a puck. They then stop, skate backward around the circle in the pattern diagramed, and pivot back to forward skating.
3. Once skating forward, the puck carrier passes and receives one-time passes from two sources as diagramed and finishes with a one-time shot on net.
4. Once the shot is completed, the shooter replaces corner passer who rejoins the closest group.
5. Players from groups *C* and *D* begin when the coach blows the next whistle.

KEY POINTS

- This is both a skill-enhancing and conditioning drill that will test the most advanced players.
- Players should attempt to pass and receive in a one-time motion whenever possible to improve the flow and tempo of the drill.

DRILL PROGRESSIONS

- Add extra passers along the skating route to increase difficulty.
- Have a second puck available for shooter in the corner who skates back to the opposite end for another shot, passing and receiving from alternate groups to the far end of the rink.

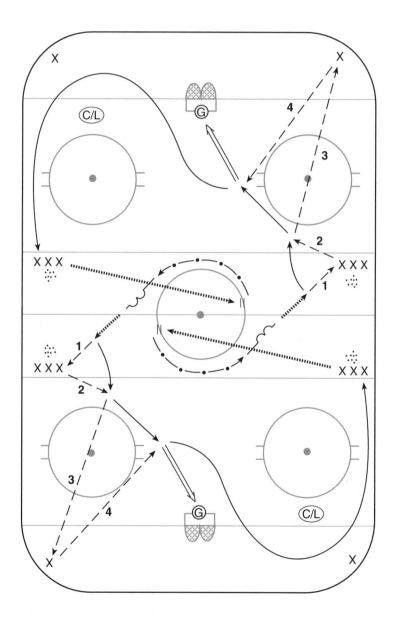

CO Boston University / Annamarie Pennucci

Deflections, Redirects, and Dekes

Teaching offensive skills can be a difficult task for any coach in any sport. We often hear coaches lament that you can teach players how to be great defenders but that great offensive players are born, not developed.

We beg to differ on this point!

Although it is true that not all players will necessarily have the elusive great instincts for offensive play, most athletes can at least improve the technical aspects of this part of their game. How? In this chapter, the focus is on developing offensive skills close to the net area and goaltender. As noted in chapter 3, the red zone is a prime location for accurate shooters and skilled offensive players to make their mark. Often, goals are scored not from dynamic end-to-end rushes but instead from close-in deflections or redirection of the puck in many key locations around the crease area.

A deflection is simply touching a puck with your stick to alter the course of a shot that has been directed toward the opposition goaltender, making a save very difficult. Players often refer to a tip-in as a shot that is raised off the ice and then deflected. Luck or chance plays a part when deflecting a puck because you cannot be certain of where it will end up.

A redirection, on the other hand, is an effort to change the route of the puck that has been shot or passed so that it will go to a specific location. Often a fine line exists between a one-time shot and a redirection when you are close to the net.

Developing Scoring Skills at the Net

The art of deflecting a puck, or making the right move at the right time in a 1-on-1 situation with the goalie, is a skill that can be learned, worked at, and improved upon. The drills in this chapter put the attackers at a distinct advantage, with the emphasis on putting the puck in the net at all cost. Offensive skills such as shooting and scoring can first be taught and then reinforced during practice and game situations. Be forewarned that because of the offensive advantage in some of the drills in this chapter, they can be demoralizing for goaltenders and defensemen if you fail to explain or understand the objectives. For example, as a coach who is gearing a practice toward these types of offensive situations, you should always acknowledge the difficulty and frustration that defenders will possibly experience. It is also important to tell defenders that they will fail in their responsibilities during some of these activities; however, this does not mean that they should begin taking shortcuts or cheat to contain attacking players. These types of attitudes can lead to poor habits on defense, something that no player or team can afford. In attempting to develop offensive skills in front of the net, consider the following important points.

Keep Your Stick Blade Close to the Ice

Ideally, any time you are near the opponent's net, your stick should remain on the ice to maximize your chances of scoring off a deflection or redirect. This is important the higher the level you play in because coaches will stress the need to keep shots low whenever a screen opportunity occurs. Certainly, players won't be able to do this all the time because defenders will try to clear the front of the net for their goaltender, and sticks will inevitably leave the ice surface. But if you concentrate on this simple concept, additional scoring chances will arise in redirections, deflections, and rebounds.

Work the Offensive Triangle

When trying to deflect point shots, you will find that working the offensive triangle is a sound way to maximize goal-scoring chances. By spreading the three attacking forwards into a triangle position, three objectives are met. First, the lead middle player sets a screen that makes the first save more difficult for the goaltender. Second, the "weak side" player is positioned to deflect or redirect any errant shots. The weak side is the area away from the puck, while the strong side is the area in which the puck is located. And third, the remaining offensive player is ready for any strong-side rebounds while also being available to retrieve any shots that miss the net on that side of the ice.

Alter the Angle of the Stick Blade

If the opposition goaltender uses a butterfly style (down on both knees quickly to cover the bottom portions of the net), deflections should be attempted into the top portions of the net. These deflections are made by changing the angle of the blade relative to the ice surface—tilting the blade back. Depending on goaltender location and position, an offensive player will sometimes merely wish to redirect a puck either left or right, as opposed to deflecting it into the upper parts of the net. This can be achieved by simply varying the position of the stick and blade as the shot arrives.

Present the Puck From the "Shooter's Position"

One-on-one with a goalie is an exciting aspect of play in hockey. The first basic concept that any attacking player should remember during a breakaway or 1-on-1 situation is to "freeze" the goalie by presenting the puck as if you are ready to shoot. This way, you can either deke or shoot, and the goalie can only guess which option is about to be used. The goaltender also will have no idea as to which side you are headed if indeed your decision is to deke. In other words—advantage shooter!

Conversely, players that stickhandle the puck in front of their bodies during a breakaway or deke situation are advertising to the goalie that a deke is coming, so the goalie only has to guess in which direction. The result is still advantage shooter, but now it is less of an advantage. Why? Because if a shot is the best option, then the puck must be drawn from the front of the body to the side for a shot, and such a move takes time to execute. Also, if you overhandle the puck in front of your body, you are apt to lose control of the puck, especially in situations in which the ice conditions are not ideal, as in the latter stages of a period or game. Keep it simple by keeping all your options open: Have the puck in the ready position for a shot.

Master One Good Move

Don't try to do too much too soon when dekeing a goaltender. Even the greatest players of all time started out with one simple move and worked from there. If the situation should arise during a game in which you are alone against a goalie, it will be important that you feel comfortable and know exactly what you intend to do with the deke. Establish one great move, then practice to add different variations to your 1-on-1 skills.

Use Goalie's Position to Determine Your Best Option

Goalies have a game plan to stop incoming shooters, as much as a pure goal scorer hates to admit it! The goaltender's objective is to outguess an attacking player using visual cues provided by the attacker during

1-on-1 confrontations. For the attacking player, there are also visual cues provided by the goalie that, if identified, can greatly improve the chances for scoring.

Key among these is goalie location in the crease. As a general rule, the farther back in the net a goalie remains as you approach, the better the opportunity to shoot during a breakaway situation. When the goalie stays back in the net, more scoring area is visible (remember telescoping?). But if the goalie appears to be coming out of the net early and challenging, the attacker should consider dekeing as a better option. The key in either case is for the attacking player to have her eyes on the goalie, not on the puck.

Check also to see that the goalie has taken a proper angle during the 1-on-1 confrontation. Sometimes in the heat of battle, a goaltender will wander too far away from either goal post and present a greater-than-normal portion of the net to shoot at. When these opportunities arise, you must be quick to make a decision and locate the puck on-target as quickly as possible.

These visual cues happen very quickly on the ice, and executing some of these techniques is easier said than done, especially for younger players. But with practice you will eventually be able to identify goalie location, position, and situation to your advantage while moving in for a scoring chance.

Learn and refine these concepts so that they become second nature during a game. Opportunities for deflections or breakaways often occur quickly, and players must be prepared to capitalize on them. The drills in this chapter will assist you in developing these important goal-scoring skills.

51 DEKE SHOWDOWN

PURPOSE

- To practice deke moves on goalies from different angles of attack

EQUIPMENT   None

TIME   3-5 minutes

PROCEDURE — Half-Ice Drill

1. Players are split into three lines in the neutral zone, pucks at each line.
2. Player from line one moves in from a side angle with a puck and attempts to deke the goalie, followed by a player from line two who skates straight at the goalie before deking. A player from line three finishes the drill with a deke from the other side of the rink.
3. Players rotate into other lines once their turn is completed.

KEY POINTS

- It is important that the goaltender be allowed to get ready for the next rush, so players should wait until the deke immediately before theirs is finished.
- This activity forces skaters and goalies to work on 1-on-1 confrontations using a variety of angles and speeds.

DRILL PROGRESSIONS

- Turn the drill into a conditioning activity for the skaters by including a skating route to be completed after each deke.
- Add a backchecker in each line who will pressure the player who is about to deke (see diagram).

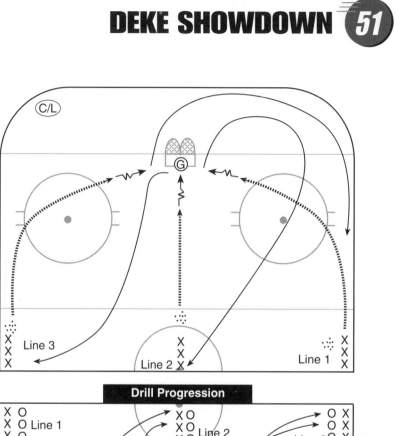

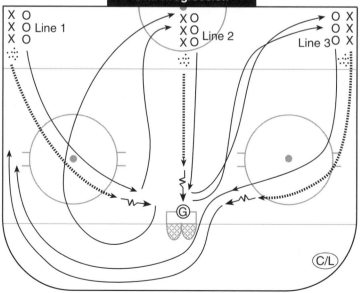

52 DOUBLE-END DEKES

PURPOSE

- To improve puck-control skills and decision making in breakaway situations.

EQUIPMENT   None

TIME   5-7 minutes

PROCEDURE — Full-Ice Drill

1. Players are situated along one of the sideboards in two groups. A group of three backcheckers is at either end along the goal line.
2. On the coach's whistle, one player from each group retrieves a puck and skates in for a deke on the goalie. After finishing this first deke, the player then skates back to the center circle to get another puck and attempt a deke on the other goalie at the opposite end of the rink.
3. A checker from the goal line chases the player as the second deke is attempted.
4. Checker goes to a dekeing line and dekers become checkers once the drill is completed.

KEY POINTS

- Players must develop essential puck-control skills to avoid losing the puck under pressure.
- To assess the best scoring option, players should be looking at the goalie, not down at the puck, as the deke is about to be made.

DRILL PROGRESSIONS

- To include a conditioning factor, make it a three-deke drill, which forces the player to skate at top speed for three full lengths of the ice.
- Designate the type of deke to be used by specific players such as on the backhand only, finishing high in the net, etc.
- Keep score, with the losing team "rewarded" with additional skating!

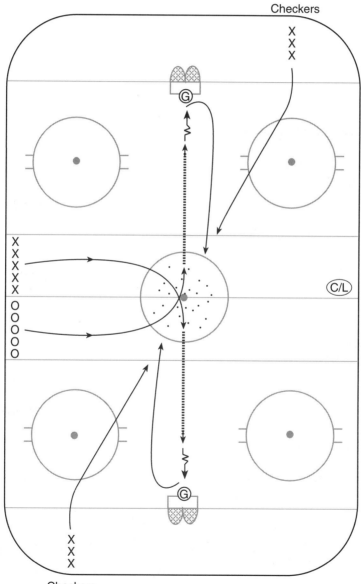

 **AIRMAIL**

PURPOSE

- To practice timing and hand-eye coordination for deflecting a puck out of the air

EQUIPMENT   None

TIME   3-5 minutes

PROCEDURE — Half-Ice Drill

1. Forwards are in two equal groups in the corners of the rink with pucks, while defensemen are split into two groups near opposite sides of the blue line as diagramed.
2. Forward from one corner passes to closest defenseman and skates toward the net. Forward might also pivot and skate backward depending on the coach's preference.
3. The defenseman releases a shot that arrives near the net at approximately waist level, and the forward must attempt to deflect it into the goal.
4. Once one side has gone, a player from the other corner starts, and the drill is repeated.

KEY POINTS

- Forwards must remember to keep the stick below the shoulder area to be a legal deflection.
- Defensemen can practice skating across the blue line with the puck before releasing the shot.
- Timing between the two is key.

DRILL PROGRESSIONS

- Have forwards skate from both corners at the same time with the defenseman deciding which player to use, while the other forward looks for any potential rebound (see diagram).
- Use a defender in front of the net to make the deflection more difficult.

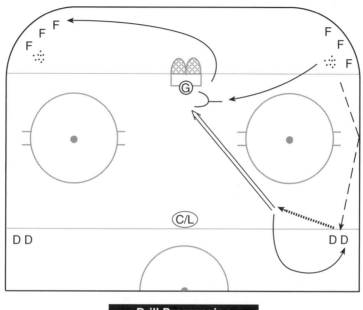

Drill Progression

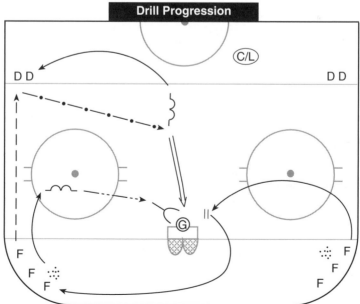

AIRMAIL 2-ON-1

PURPOSE

- To practice deflections and redirects leading to an offensive attack

EQUIPMENT   None

TIME   3-5 minutes

PROCEDURE — Full-Ice Drill

1. A variation of Drill #53.
2. Forwards are in all four corners near the hash marks, with pucks, in equal numbers. Defensemen are split into two groups at opposite sides of the blue lines as shown.
3. Play begins in one end when one forward passes to a defenseman, then skates to the front of the net. Defenseman skates along the blue line and shoots a puck that is deflected by the forward.
4. Forward continues skating after deflection toward the opposite boards, where player from the other line feeds a pass and the two begin a 2-on-1 rush against the defenseman who shot the puck initially. Drill begins from the other end after first rush is completed.

KEY POINTS

- Forward who is deflecting should stay in motion while cutting across the front of the net, making this a timing drill. Momentum is therefore maintained as the 2-on-1 begins.

DRILL PROGRESSIONS

- Allow the other forward to skate toward the net and act as a redirect option for the defenseman shooting the puck.
- Position another defenseman in front of the net to clear for the goalie.

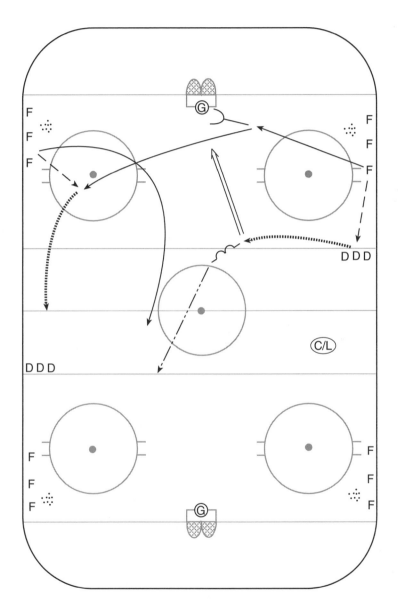

QUIET-ZONE REDIRECT

PURPOSE

- To practice redirect skills in the offensive zone off a cycle play

EQUIPMENT   None

TIME   4-5 minutes

PROCEDURE — Half-Ice Drill

1. Play must occur below the tops of the face-off circles or hash marks (leader's discretion).
2. Players are in two lines with the first pair moving to attack as the coach directs a puck into either corner.
3. Player with puck begins skating away from the net area along the boards, then reverses the play by backpassing to partner positioned behind the net.
4. Second player then skates along the boards while first player skates to front/side of the net and redirects a pass into the net.
5. Players then return to the back of the opposite line for the next attack.

KEY POINTS

- Player shooting puck toward the net is not trying to score but rather put a hard pass on the stick of the other player for a redirection.
- Player who is deflecting must keep the stick low to the ice and have good body position to effect the best possible tip or redirect.

DRILL PROGRESSIONS

- Have three lines and two options for the shooter, either a deflection or a redirect (see diagram).
- Add late pressure to both passer and redirecting player to increase speed of the drill.

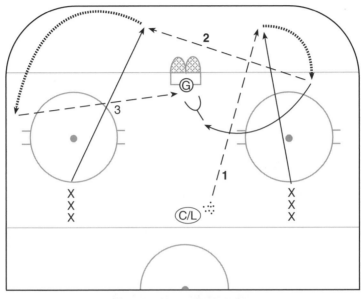

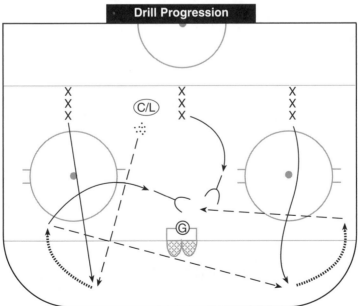

Drill Progression

56 JAM CITY

PURPOSE

- To practice goal-scoring activities tight to the net, including redirects

EQUIPMENT   None

TIME   4-5 minutes

PROCEDURE — Half-Ice Drill

1. Players are located in one of two lines at the top of the face-off circles.
2. Coach puts a puck behind the net with a player from one of the lines retrieving it while a player from the other line skates wide around the face-off circle and into the corner.
3. Player with puck then skates to the front of the net and can either attempt to jam it home or make a quick pass across the goal crease to the other player for a redirect.
4. Players then return to the back of the opposite line for the next attack.

KEY POINTS

- Another timing drill that forces partners to learn when to move and when to delay.
- Player with the puck should attempt to confuse the goalie, using head and stick fakes so the goaltender is not sure where the puck is headed.

DRILL PROGRESSIONS

- Add a defender at the blue line who will shoot a second puck for tip-in opportunities after the first puck has been played (see diagram).
- Remove the goaltender's stick to allow forwards the chance to become proficient.
- Finish the drill with a conditioning skate.

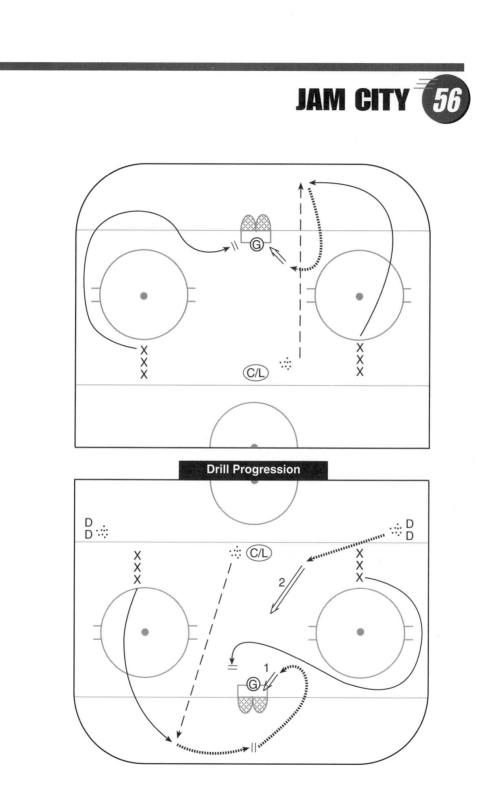

Drill Progression

THREE-LINE REDIRECTS & TIPS

PURPOSE

- To practice tip-in and redirect skills

EQUIPMENT   None

TIME   3-5 minutes

PROCEDURE — Half-Ice Drill

1. Players are in one of three lines in the neutral zone with pucks.
2. Play begins by having a player in line one carry a puck toward the sideboards near line two. A player from line two slowly moves into the middle ice area with a puck as the line one player moves past and into the attack zone.
3. Player from line one skates wide, shoots a puck on net, and then follows for a tip-in or redirect from player in line two, who is now skating into the mid-ice area. Line three shooter delays until second shooter is at the net after the second shot and then attempts a shot or pass, which may be tipped or redirected by either of the first two shooters.

KEY POINTS

- Timing is again important as players learn to buy time until teammates are in a position to tip or redirect.
- Players who are redirecting or deflecting should remember to call for the puck as the player sets up to shoot.

DRILL PROGRESSIONS

- Try a double redirect in which the puck is redirected between two players in the same sequence, a very difficult skill.
- Have additional pucks behind the net for a second shot opportunity off a wraparound (see diagram).
- Add some defensive pressure to make things more difficult for attackers.

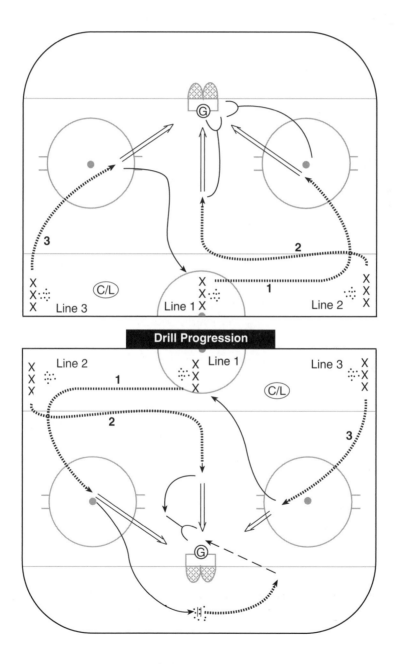

Drill Progression

58 THREE-LINE ESCAPE

PURPOSE

- To practice puck control and timing, leading to a tip-in or redirect opportunity

EQUIPMENT   None

TIME   3-4 minutes

PROCEDURE — Half-Ice Drill

1. A follow-up activity for Drill #57.
2. Players are in one of three lines in the neutral zone with pucks. A supply of pucks is also in the corners.
3. Line one player along the boards begins with a long shot from the blue line area, then skates to the corner, retrieves another puck, and initiates an escape move up the sideboards. Player in line two delays until line one player is out of the escape move, then line two player moves in for a one-time shot off a pass from line one player.
4. Player two continues to opposite corner, retrieves a puck, and passes to line three player who has delayed before joining the attack. This player then attempts a pass/shot toward player one who has skated to the front/side of the net.

KEY POINTS

- Players two and three must be patient and not get into the play too quickly because timing is a critical element.
- Try to make passes as crisp and accurate as possible to guarantee offensive success.

DRILL PROGRESSIONS

- Make the drill a 3-on-1 and allow different options for puck carriers at the various stages of the drill (e.g., may shoot or go to the back of the net).
- Have all three players regroup after the last shot is taken, retrieve a puck between the red and blue lines, and run a 3-on-0 to add a second offensive component to the drill (see diagram).

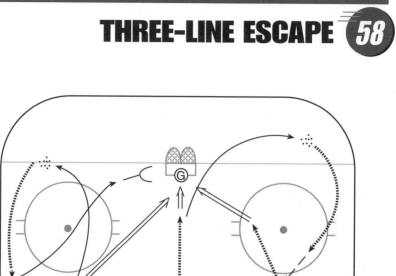

Drill Progression

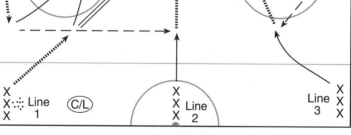

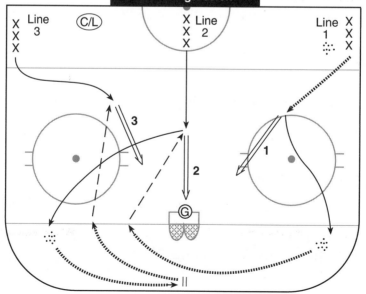

59 THREE-LINE DELAY

PURPOSE

- To practice full ice attacks on net, finishing with tip-in or redirect opportunities

EQUIPMENT   None

TIME   3-4 minutes

PROCEDURE — Full-Ice Drill

1. Players are in two equal groups at opposite diagonal ends of the rink with pucks.
2. In groups of three, players from one group begin skating in a staggered fashion toward the opposite end of the rink.
3. After crossing the blue line, player one shoots the puck from the side, then follows to the net and stops, waiting for a tip-in, redirect, or rebound from player two, who has timed his attack so that the shot arrives at the net at the same time as player one. Both players one and two then wait for player three to complete the drill with a shot on net.
4. When all three have shot, the next group begins skating from the other end.

KEY POINTS

- This is another drill that forces players to become aware of the timing required when entering a play as they attempt to redirect or tip a puck.
- Good activity for goalies who must always concentrate on the first shot yet be prepared to move laterally for leg saves.

DRILL PROGRESSIONS

- Have a defenseman come across the blue line to finish the drill, shooting through a three-player screen that is difficult for the goalie.
- Players could use the opposite group as a passing option as they enter the zone before shooting.

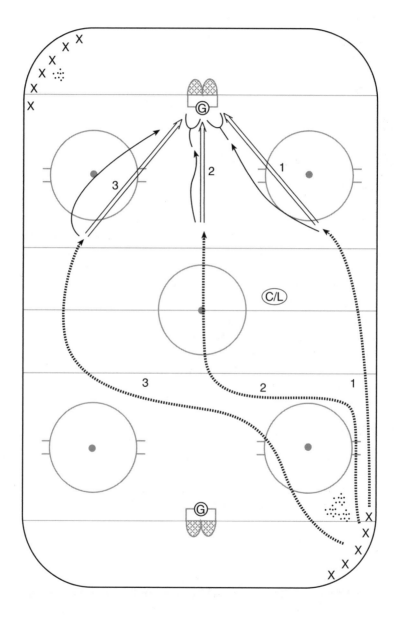

SATOR'S TRANSITION

PURPOSE

- To practice regrouping out of the offensive zone, leading to a tip-in or redirect opportunity

EQUIPMENT   None

TIME   8-10 minutes

PROCEDURE — Full-Ice Drill

1. Defensemen are in one of two groups at either blue line. Forwards are evenly distributed to all four corners with pucks.
2. Play begins with a forward passing to a defenseman at the blue line, who skates along the line before shooting on net. One forward from each group in that end goes to the net for a tip-in, rebound, or redirect.
3. Coach then places a puck behind the defenseman in either the neutral zone or far blue line area that the defenseman must retrieve after skating backward and pivoting. Forwards exit zone while this is happening and position themselves to receive an outlet pass from the defenseman.
4. Once the pass is received, the forwards finish the drill with the second shot on net, then play begins from the other end in a similar fashion.

KEY POINTS

- Forwards must vacate the zone quickly and be onside to accept the second puck.
- Forwards must remember to stay onside as puck is delivered.
- Defensemen must get over the blue line before passing so as to avoid a two-line passing violation.

DRILL PROGRESSIONS

- Use an entire line (three players) for the drill.
- Have the defenseman follow the play on the second puck and shoot the puck after receiving a return pass from forwards. This will allow for a redirect or deflection chance.

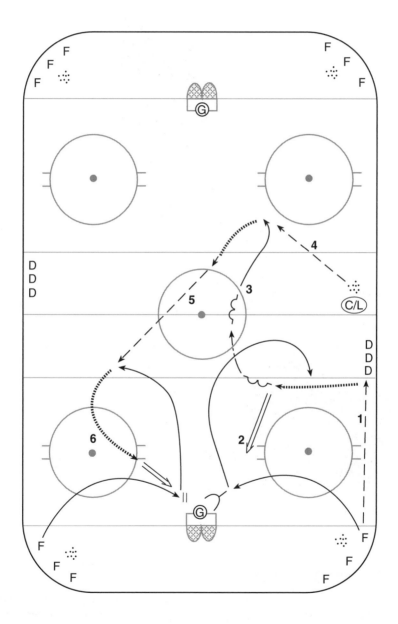

8 Mastering Scoring Techniques

Several years ago, a Huron instructor stood in front of a group of eager young players during a hockey school session and asked, "How many of you would like to make a comfortable living playing hockey in the NHL?" Of course, every hand was raised. He then asked, "How many of you want more than a comfortable living in the NHL? How many want to be a multimillionaire by playing in the NHL?" Every hand was raised again, this time with greater enthusiasm. The coach then responded, "Well, for you players who want to make a comfortable living, go see coach Smith, and he'll teach you how to be a defensive specialist. The rest of you who want to be multimillionaires, stay with me. . . . I'm going to teach you how to become a goal scorer!!"

It seems true that in virtually every sport, the glamour players—the offensive threats—receive most of the acclaim and financial rewards. Although we cannot guarantee anyone who reads this book millionaire status, let alone a comfortable living as an NHL player, we can provide elite-level drilling as seen in this chapter that will help push you further along on your shooting and scoring developmental path.

Most coaches would cringe at the thought of an entire team of players in which everyone is striving only to score goals. Obviously, teams need balance, with different players offering different specialties. But coaches do require players who can finish scoring chances—after all, the team with the most goals wins. And by improving this aspect of your play, you present another option for yourself, your coach, and your team.

The drills contained in the following pages will test the greatest talents in the world. Although they may not necessarily be the most complex of drills, they nevertheless act as accurate benchmarks for player development. When you can execute the drills in this chapter at top speed with precision and confidence, you will be on your way to scoring mastery.

Remember that developing scoring skills takes years to perfect. Your outcome should be the ability to replicate the skills taught in this book on a consistent basis at high speed, over an extended period of time, and under game conditions.

61 CENTER RETREATS

PURPOSE

- To develop foot speed and puck-handling skills leading to a shooting opportunity

EQUIPMENT   None

TIME   5-6 minutes

PROCEDURE — Half-Ice Drill

1. Players are in the center face-off area with a supply of pucks.
2. Coach blows a whistle, and two players begin the drill by skating in opposite directions around the circle with a puck.
3. Players must pivot, skate backward away from the circle, pivot again, and finish with a crossover turn before moving in for a shot on net.
4. After the shot is taken, players follow for any rebound chances and then vacate the zone at top speed, returning to the center ice area.
5. Alternate shooting sides by starting the drill on opposite sides of the circle.

KEY POINTS

- To execute this type of activity at top speed takes great skill because of the many actions involved.
- Players should attempt to keep the head focused forward, not down, as a means of mastery during this activity.

DRILL PROGRESSIONS

- Create a give-and-go situation throughout the drill with the next person in line by passing every three or four strides.
- Provide shooting options for the player, such as cutting to the middle, moving in for a deke, attempting a wraparound, etc.
- Have the two players involved compete for a second puck that is placed randomly on the ice, creating a second-shot opportunity.

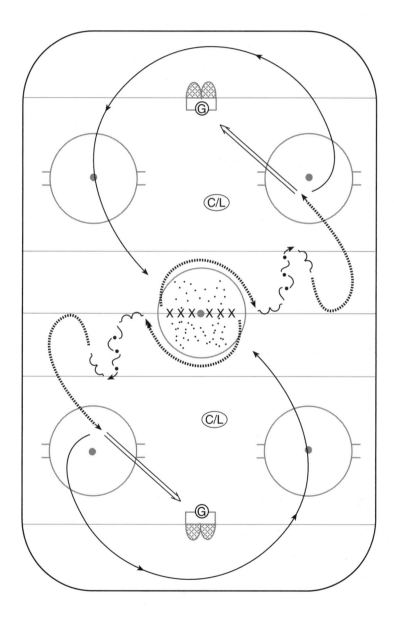

62 THE WEAVE

PURPOSE

- To practice maintaining puck control through passing at a very high speed, resulting in a scoring opportunity

EQUIPMENT   None

TIME   4-5 minutes total

PROCEDURE — Full-Ice Drill

1. Players are in one of three lines at either end of the rink.
2. Drill begins with middle-lane player skating forward with a puck and initiating a pass to a player on either side, then skating in the same direction of the pass and cutting behind the player who received the pass.
3. Additional passes are made as the players skate the length of the rink, each time having the passer skate in the direction of the pass and cutting behind the receiver.
4. Play is finished with a shot on goal, and three new players begin the drill again heading in the opposite direction.
5. The three players who complete the drill stay in that end and move into one of the three lines for a return trip down the ice.

KEY POINTS

- This is similar to one of the staple drills used in basketball, and it forces players to accelerate to keep the play flowing.
- Player receiving the pass can help by cutting toward the passer, making for an easy transition from one side to the other.

DRILL PROGRESSIONS

- Try this drill with two pucks!
- Attempt the activity while skating backward the length of the ice.
- Add a regroup feature and run three line weaves consecutively with the same group.

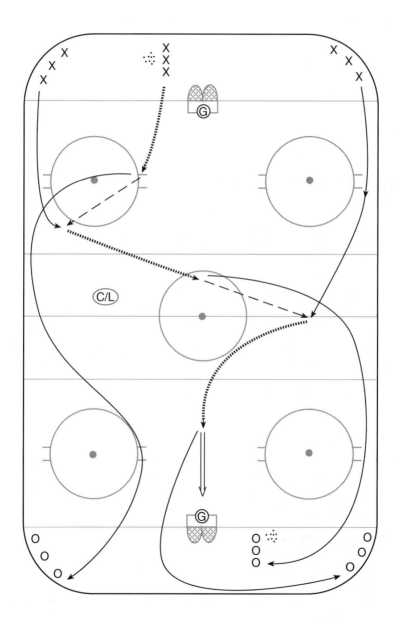

63 THREE-RUSH THROTTLE

PURPOSE

- To create goal-scoring opportunities for offensive units (lines) while skating at top speed

EQUIPMENT   None

TIME   5 minutes

- 20-25 seconds per three rushes

PROCEDURE — Full-Ice Drill

1. Drill begins at the players' bench, with players sitting with their line mates; defensemen form groups of three as well. Pucks are at either end, spread out between the end boards and the goal lines.
2. On coach's whistle, one line jumps over the boards to enter the ice, and the play begins with one player skating to the goal line to retrieve a puck. A pass is immediately made to a line mate, and the three players initiate a full-ice 3-on-0, ending with a shot on goal.
3. One of the three players then retrieves a second puck from below the goal line, and all three loop and skate 3-on-0 toward the other end. They must finish this rush with a different offensive play than the one used on the previous rush.
4. The sequence finishes in a similar fashion with a third and different offensive play.

KEY POINTS

- Once the line finishes the third rush, the next line jumps the boards to begin the cycle again.
- High speed is critical, and each rush has to finish differently; it's time for creativity!

DRILL PROGRESSIONS

- Add a defenseman at each blue line to shoot a second puck after each rush.
- Designate a minimum number of passes between line mates during each attack.

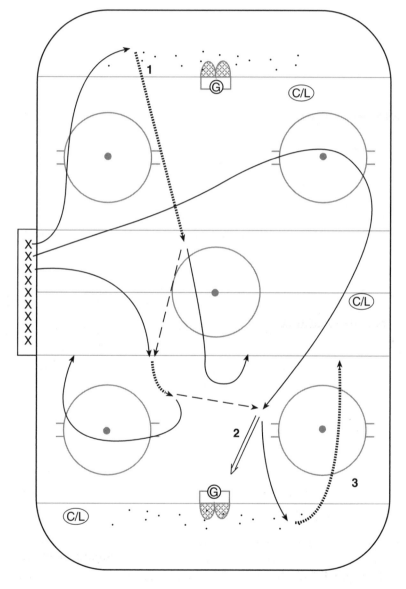

BULLET SCREENS

PURPOSE

- To practice shooting through a screen situation
- To condition the athletes

EQUIPMENT   None

TIME   3-4 minutes

PROCEDURE — Full-Ice Drill

1. Forwards are tight to one sideboard area in the neutral zone with defensemen lined up directly in front of them. Pucks are at either end, spread out between the endboards and the goal line.
2. One forward loops to an end and receives a pass from a coach in a corner, turns, and skates toward the opposite end of the ice. At the same time, a defenseman has joined the play and presents a 1-on-1 situation.
3. Once in the other zone, the forward uses the defenseman as a screen on the goalie and attempts to shoot through the legs or between the stick and feet.
4. Once the shot is taken, the defenseman turns, picks up a puck located near the end boards, and feeds a pass to another forward who is beginning the play again headed in the opposite direction. Another defenseman skates in to create the 1-on-1, and the drill continues.

KEY POINTS

- This drill should be done at high speed.
- The forward may attempt to beat the defenseman on the 1-on-1 if at an advantage, but the main purpose is to use a screen situation.

DRILL PROGRESSIONS

- Use the same procedure to turn this into a 2-on-2 situation.
- Add a trailing player who will pressure the attacker from behind.
- Remember to switch sides; try having the goalie make the clearing pass!

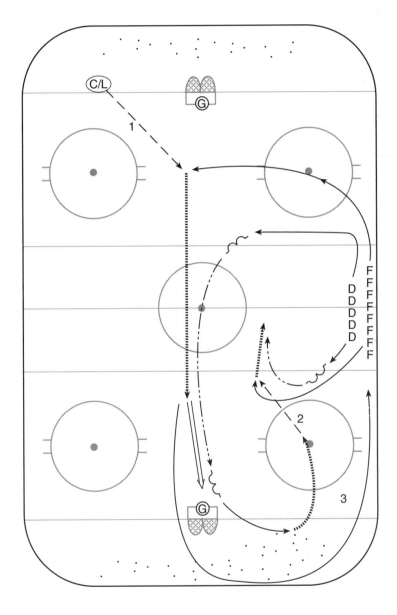

HIT THE HOLE 2-ON-0

PURPOSE

- To provide practice for defensemen in outlet passing technique and joining the offensive attack

EQUIPMENT   4 pylons

TIME   3-4 minutes

PROCEDURE — Full-Ice Drill

1. Drill will start from both ends when the coach's whistle is blown.
2. Forwards are together in one of two groups designated *A*, at opposite corners of the rink, with defensemen in two groups designated as *B*, also in opposite corners.
3. A defenseman skates toward the corner and receives a pass from the second defenseman in line, performs an escape move, and passes to a forward who begins the drill at the same time. The forward comes from the corner and skates across the ice surface looking for a breakout pass.
4. The defenseman joins the attack quickly, making it a 2-on-0 situation.
5. Once shot is taken, the whistle is blown, and new players continue the activity.

KEY POINTS

- Forwards must time the drill to allow defensemen an opportunity to catch up to the play.
- Defensemen must pass and skate immediately if they hope to be a part of the offensive rush.

DRILL PROGRESSIONS

- Another whistle during the drill would signify a regroup option, meaning that players would circle and skate in the opposite direction to finish the drill, ending with a shot on goal.
- Add a defender who skates from the center circle as the 2-on-0 enters the offensive zone, adding pressure to the activity.

HIT THE HOLE 2-ON-0 65

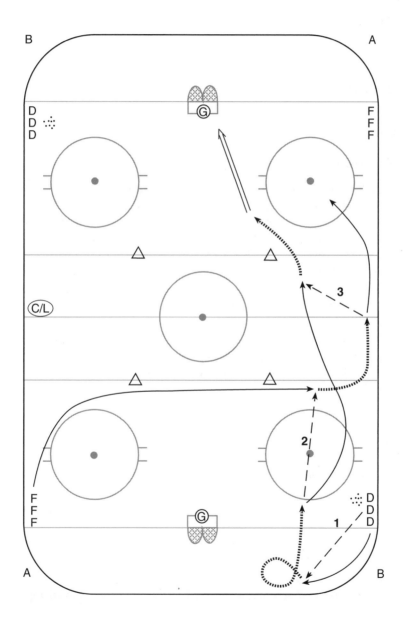

66 WALSH'S 2-ON-1

PURPOSE

- To practice outnumbered situations leading to a goal-scoring opportunity

EQUIPMENT   None

TIME   4-5 minutes

PROCEDURE — Full-Ice Drill

1. Forwards and defensemen are evenly divided in four groups, two each at opposite ends of the rink; defenders have pucks. Defensemen are situated along the goal line, and forwards are near the face-off circle hash marks in their respective groups.
2. Coach blows the whistle, and play begins out of both ends at once with a defenseman carrying a puck behind the net.
3. Simultaneously, two forwards cut across ice and begin to skate toward the opposite end after one has received a pass from the defenseman.
4. The defenseman must then skate quickly to the near blue line, pivot, and skate backward to defend against the two forwards who are coming from the opposite end of the rink, completing a 2-on-1 sequence.

KEY POINTS

- Forwards should be moving at top speed to try to catch the defenseman at a disadvantage and finish the play with a good scoring chance.
- Attacking players should attempt to determine the best chance to beat the defenseman based on the defender's alignment and positioning.

DRILL PROGRESSIONS

- Another whistle would signify a regroup in which the defenseman would have to skate up ice and handle the other pair of forwards in a 2-on-1.
- Add a second puck by the side of the net, which forwards attempt to retrieve after the first shot for an additional scoring chance.

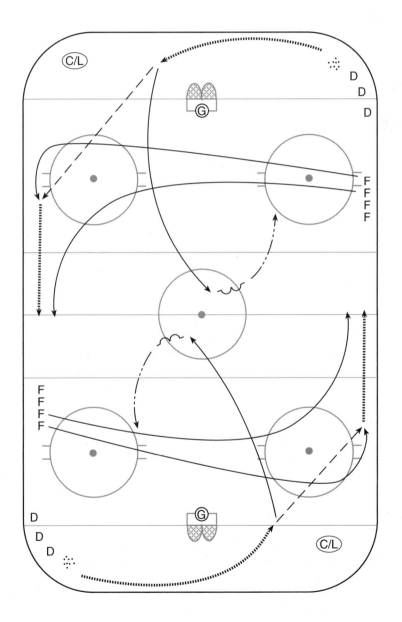

67 BACKCHECK 3-ON-2

PURPOSE

- To force players to gain control and pass as quickly as possible for a scoring opportunity

EQUIPMENT   None

TIME   4-5 minutes

PROCEDURE — Full-Ice Drill

1. Forward lines are positioned in three equal groups in the neutral zone as shown, with defensemen prepared to play a half-ice 3-on-2. Four defensemen, situated at either blue line, start the play.
2. A coach who is positioned near the red line with pucks will put one into either end, and the group of forwards begin an attack. Defensemen must start at the same time as the attacking forwards, skating backward to the top of the face-off circles, which provides an advantage to the forwards.
3. When the whistle blows, coach will place a puck in the opposite end, signifying a 3-on-2 for that end to begin.
4. The forward highest or closest to the blue line in the end where the drill was initiated must retreat and become a backchecker in the opposite end, making the drill a 3-on-3 as it concludes.

KEY POINTS

- Do this drill at a high speed, simulating a backcheck effort during game conditions.
- The forwards on the attack must make quick decisions and execute a shot before the backchecker gets into position to defend.

DRILL PROGRESSIONS

- Have all the remaining players from the initial end join the second groups of forwards with designated roles, making it a 5-on-5.
- Have the initial group complete the first part of the drill by playing out the 2-on-2 situation; add a late player from the bench area to create a 3-on-2 offensive situation.

BACKCHECK 3-ON-2 67

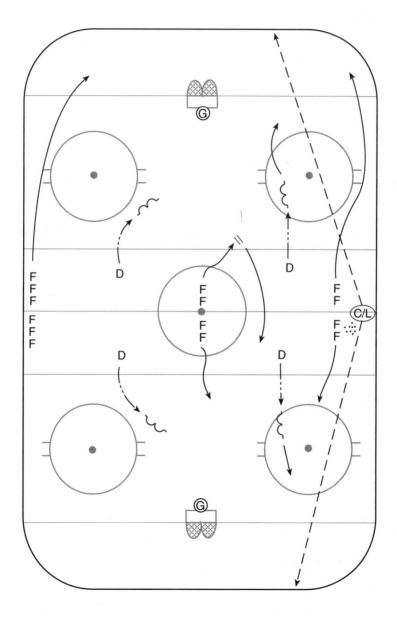

COWBOY'S DELIGHT

PURPOSE

- To teach players the concepts of timing, width, and depth in an offensive attack

EQUIPMENT   4 pylons

TIME   4-5 minutes

PROCEDURE — Full-Ice Drill

1. Players are in one of four groups near the sideboards at the blue lines. Four pylons are placed along the blue lines as shown, near each of the face-off dots in the neutral zone between the two blue lines.
2. A group of three players from group one skates toward the goal at the far end of the rink with two players having to stay on the outside of either pylon when approaching the far blue line. The third player skates through the middle of the ice.
3. One player from group one receives a puck from a player in the group directly across on the opposite side of the ice (group three) and skates deep into the corner. A tight turn or escape move is then executed, and the puck carrier looks to make a pass.
4. The middle skater goes directly to the front of the net and is the first pass option, while the second player delays by skating parallel to the blue line and then heads for the net.
5. A pass is made and a shot taken. A player from group four then begins the drill in the opposite direction.

KEY POINTS

- This activity forces players to be patient and work for a best shot opportunity, using all the offensive ice surface in the process.
- Take time before the drill begins to explain options and reasons for "center penetration."

DRILL PROGRESSIONS

- This drill can be expanded into a cycling activity if the puck carrier elects not to pass. Players cycle the puck along the sideboards until a good pass can be made into the red zone for a shot opportunity.
- Add one or two defenders who attempt to restrict passing options.

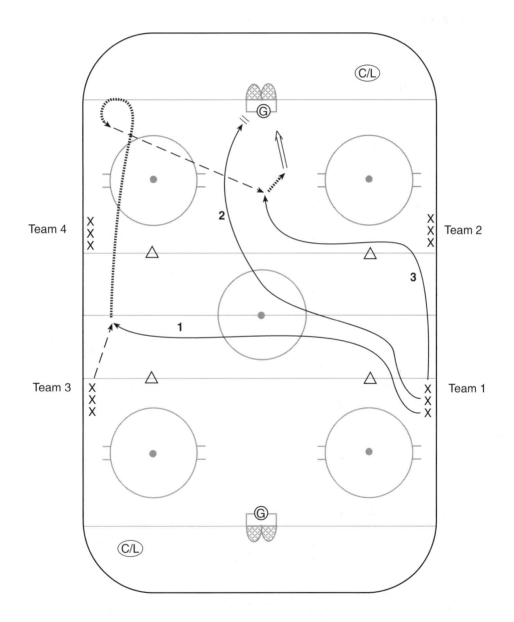

 **SPITFIRE CYCLE**

PURPOSE

- To develop a puck-control situation that leads to a quality scoring option off a pass

EQUIPMENT   None

TIME   4-5 minutes

- 20 seconds per group

PROCEDURE — Half-Ice Drill

1. Players are in groups of three in a triangle position in a corner at either end. The coach has pucks and is in the mid-ice area between the tops of the face-off circles. Extra players stay near the coach waiting for their turn.
2. A puck is placed in the corner; one of the three players retrieves it and begins to move along the sideboards toward the neutral zone area.
3. Player then backpasses in opposite direction to the corner, and the next player retrieves.
4. Once a player has cycled to the corner, he or she must loop toward the front of the net for a potential shot opportunity. Players rotate in a circular fashion until a pass is made from the corner and a shot occurs.
5. Coach then places another puck in the opposite corner, and three new players begin to cycle.

KEY POINTS

- Players must anticipate the cycle pass and move quickly to the puck.
- You should only do one side at a time so that goalies are not asked to face two shots arriving at the same moment from opposite corners.

DRILL PROGRESSIONS

- Designate a defensive player who will try to disrupt the cycling action. Player with the puck must then make good decisions as to whether a cycle is appropriate or whether an attack on the net is the better option (see diagram).
- Have a multiple-cycling set and alternate corners. Once a group of three shots has been taken from one side, move immediately to the other corner and run another cycle from that side as well.

SPITFIRE CYCLE 69

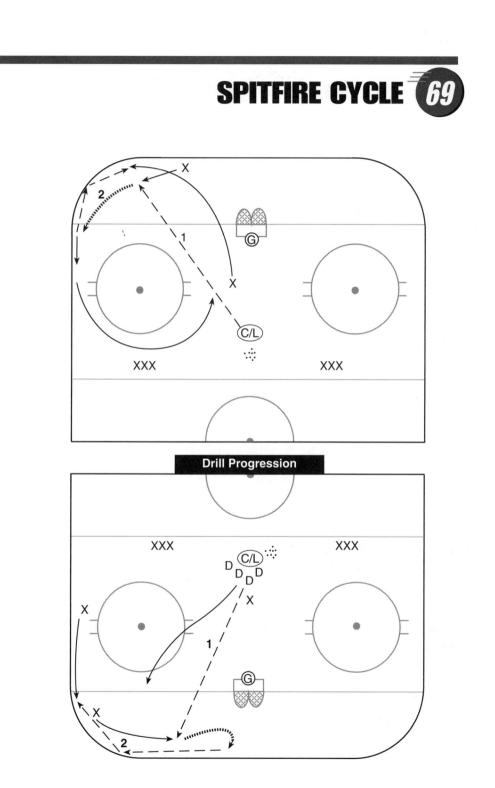

Drill Progression

MacLEAN'S ATTACK

PURPOSE

- To practice outnumbered offensive situations in a half-ice format

EQUIPMENT   None

TIME   4-5 minutes

PROCEDURE — Half-Ice Drill

1. Forwards are in the neutral zone area in one of three lines as shown.
2. Defensemen are near the center red line waiting to take their positions on either blue line about to face a 3-on-1 attack.
3. Coach puts a puck in the corner, and the defenseman must retrieve it and make an outlet pass to the closest forward.
4. All three forwards then skate back into the neutral zone to regroup, turn and attack the defenseman who originally passed the puck. Forwards must stay onside during the regroup phase.
5. Play can be done at both ends simultaneously with new groups of players starting when a goal is scored or the puck smothered by the goaltender. Players return to a different line once their line rush is completed.

KEY POINTS

- This drill allows considerable offensive work to be accomplished in a limited amount of time, focusing on decision making and finishing around the net.
- Forwards must regroup at high speed, making sure to stay onside as the attack develops.

DRILL PROGRESSIONS

- Add a second defenseman and begin the drill with a D-to-D pass, simulating a breakout pattern, then make it a half-ice 3-on-2 activity (see diagram).
- Have a second puck option for the forwards after the first rush is completed.

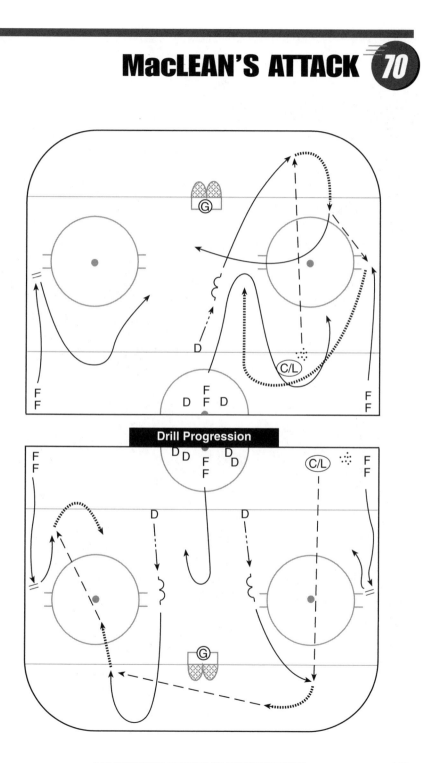

Drill Progression

Sample Practice Sessions

To give you an idea of how to structure a practice using the activities in this book, we have provided some sample practice plans. When designing an effective practice session, coaches and players should first consider the following important factors.

- **Take time to prepare.** Have a general "game plan" for each practice session, and share the objectives for that specific practice with players. Most players want to improve and want to please their coaches, but it is difficult to do either of those if players do not understand what is expected of them. Always take the time to prepare, and share your ideas with the players before you hit the ice.
- **Use the entire ice surface efficiently.** Rather than running all full-ice drills, split the ice in half, thirds, or even quarters, depending on the theme for that day. Ice-time costs can be prohibitive, so it is important to make every second count toward skill development.
- **Break the team into workable groups**. Much like proper ice-time use, players should be active for as much of the time as possible while on the ice. For example, a full-ice drill in which only two players are active while 18 others stand motionless is not inclusive and is rarely worthwhile. Break the team into smaller groups so that players can repeat each drill more often in the same amount of time.
- **Consider station work to reinforce specific skills**. Station-based learning is a popular concept in classrooms across North America, so why not try it on the ice as well? If the theme is shooting and scoring, divide the team into groups, each group at its own specific drill station. Many of the drills in this book can be adapted to work in stations. Before getting into sample practice sessions, let's look at how a station-based approach works on the ice.

Three-Station Drill Session

The following example demonstrates how you might use stations as an effective means of practicing scoring for players of all ages—in this case using a three-station drill. Station work is fun for players, yet it reinforces the basics of shooting and scoring. Variations of this activity are endless, and players will quickly understand the organization and sequence they must follow. As a progression, you might consider making the following activity a partner drill, in which two players come out at the same time and try to maintain puck control between the pair, leading to a scoring chance. You'll find that by simply changing drill parameters, many of the activities in this book can work as station drills.

Guidelines for Three-Station Drills

- Split ice into thirds lengthwise, placing pylons to indicate the boundaries for each station (see diagram). Then split the team into thirds, with each group going to one station.
- An extra net should be brought on the ice so that each station can be used for scoring finishes.
- Players go through the station and return to the same starting point, *making sure not to cross into another lane* (this can be dangerous if a high-speed collision occurs).
- Players return to the line by staying tight to the pylon boundary markers, making certain not to interfere with the next person doing the drill.
- Ensure that players understand how each station is run. Demonstrate the activity if possible.
- On the whistle, players rotate as a group to the next station.
- Total time per station is approximately five minutes, meaning the entire activity will take 15 to 17 minutes total.

Deke Drill

Have a leader C standing on each blue line, forcing the oncoming player to maneuver, or "deke," while maintaining control of the puck. The person at the blue line may only skate laterally, not forward or backward. Depending on age and skill level, restrict the amount of contact—perhaps allowing only stickchecking for younger participants. Finish the drill by using another deke move on the goaltender. This drill allows players to work on using stick, shoulder, and head fakes as a way of getting open for scoring chances, while finishing with a deke as well.

Gate Drill

Put two pylons approximately five feet apart at one blue line, with a hockey stick lying on the ice approximately three to five feet directly behind them. Set up a similar "gate" at the other end directly in front of a goalie in a net. Players must skate through the pylons and cut sharply in either direction while maintaining control of the puck. If you have help on the ice, have someone stand behind the gate and point in either direction as the player approaches. The player must react quickly and go in the direction indicated by the leader. As players approach the goalie,

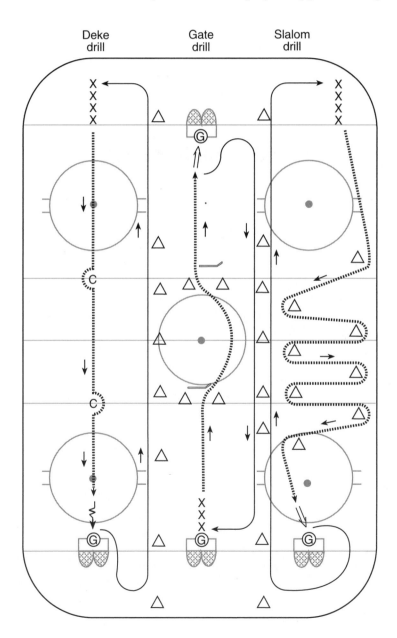

they have the option of moving either way out of the gate and releasing either a forehand or a backhand shot depending on which side they exit to. Players should follow their shots to the net for possible rebound opportunities.

Slalom

Set pylons far apart, then have a series of three or four close together, forcing players to make quick turns, much like a slalom skier. Once a player is at the red line, the next person in line may begin. The player must come out of the slalom, set the puck in the ready (shooting) position, and then decide whether to shoot or deke the goalie.

Sample Practice Plans

The following practice plans combine drills described in earlier chapters. These three examples demonstrate how you can approach one common theme—scoring—in a variety of ways and with differing specific objectives. Note that we have intentionally loaded these sessions with quite a few drills and that we spend limited amounts of time on each. You may find that with your specific group of players, fewer drills would be preferable, resulting in more time being spent on those drills you choose to incorporate in your practice. Feel free to pick, choose, modify, and adapt as you see fit.

When putting together practice plans, remember that often a drill from one topic area in the book can easily be used or substituted for another part of practice. For example, a traditional shooting activity could be used as a warm-up drill if done in such a way that the finishing aspect of the drill is not included. Experiment with different combinations, then seek feedback from players and fellow coaches about how effective a particular practice was on any given day. Never stop learning and trying new ideas. The perfect practice might be just around the corner!

For the following practices, we are assuming that coaches will add an extra five minutes for transition time between drills. Remember, too, that most rinks have 10 minutes each hour allotted for resurfacing the ice, which also cuts into drill time. In addition, five minutes has been set aside for a simple warm-up period before shooting activities begin as players enter the ice surface. In total, this means that 20 minutes out of the one-hour block is already accounted for, leaving 40 minutes of drill time. No wonder we constantly here coaches lament, "We never have enough time on the ice!"

SAMPLE PRACTICE PLAN 1

Total Time: 60 minutes

Theme: Scoring

Objective: To refine general shooting skills with no pressure

Drill Sequence	Time Required (min)

1. **DRILL #4 — The Combo** — 3
   Allows players to try different shots;
   goalies feel some rubber

2. **DRILL #12 — Full-Ice Angles** — 3
   Players shoot from different angles, long range

3. **DRILL #13 — Team Rockets** — 3
   Gets the legs moving in this full-ice activity

4. **DRILL #21 — Five-Puck Finish** — 5
   Keeps players focused on finishing at the net
   with no contact

5. **DRILL #48 — Trapshooting** — 6
   Forces players to move the feet and get to
   open areas

6. **DRILL #47 — Two-Player Dash** — 5
   A wide open skating/shooting activity

7. **DRILL #58 — Three-Line Escape** — 5
   Players work on offensive timing

8. **DRILL #20 — Empty Tank** — 5
   Finish the practice on a high note with a
   fun activity

9. **Recap, optional skate at the end, or free time** — 5

Total Activity Time — 40

SAMPLE PRACTICE PLAN 2

Total Time: 60 minutes

Theme: Scoring

Objective: To refine general scoring skills in a fun environment

Drill Sequence	Time Required (min)
1. **DRILL #16 — Razer's Edge** *Players can use this to get loose, work on angles, set goalie position in net*	4
2. **DRILL #17 — Razer's Edge II** *Why not use a progression off the first drill to guarantee some success?*	4
3. **DRILL #18 — Numbers Game** *Will invigorate the group while adding a skating dimension*	3
4. **DRILL #23 — Ladder Game** *Keeping score is optional but the players will love this*	3
5. **DRILL #25 — Coaches' Choice** *Players will enjoy the challenge of different situations during this activity*	6
6. **DRILL #27 — Safe House 3-on-3** *The safety in all corners will allow players to get into the "comfort zones"*	5
7. **DRILL #53 — Airmail** *Slow it down a bit by adding a real skill activity that works on tip-ins*	5
8. **SHOWDOWN (1-on-1 with goalie from center ice)** *This is a great way to finish any practice*	10

Total Activity Time	40

SAMPLE PRACTICE PLAN 3

Total Time: 60 minutes

Theme: Scoring

Objective: To develop pressure scoring skills and enhance player conditioning

1. **DRILL #9 — Full-Ice Loop**   4
   A good way to follow easy warm-up activities

2. **DRILL #19 — Newt's Double 'D'**   4
   Gets players ready for contact by practicing escape moves and tight turns

3. **DRILL #34 — Grunt Drill**   5
   An old reliable that will get the players into it early

4. **DRILL #32 — Grease**   3
   Players must battle for every scoring chance

5. **DRILL #33 — Grease Fire**   3
   Quickly move into the companion drill for #32

6. **DRILL #26 — Wild Card 3-on-3**   5
   Throw in a game to keep the juices flowing

7. **DRILL #40 — Beat the Box**   6
   The players will really get into this: forces great focus and concentration (plus courage!!)

8. **DRILL #54 — Airmail 2-on-1**   4
   Slow it down a bit with a simple 2-on-1 activity

9. **DRILL #24 — Survival**   6
   An exhausting drill; cool down and stretch

9. **Recap key teaching points during this time together**

Total Activity Time   40

About the Authors

Newell Brown (left) and Vern Stenlund (second from right) show two recent Huron Hockey graduates the proper way to celebrate a goal.

From his boyhood involvement at Huron Hockey camps to a coaching career in the NHL, **Newell Brown** has seemed destined for success in hockey. Prior to the 1996-97 NHL season, the then 33-year-old Brown was named an assistant coach for the Chicago Blackhawks.

His appointment came on the heels of a sterling coaching career in the Detroit Red Wings organization. From 1992 to 1996 Brown coached the top development team for the parent organization, the Adirondack Red Wings of Glen Falls, New York. In four seasons his teams won or tied 58 percent of their games and three times finished first or second in the North Division of the American Hockey League.

From 1990 to 1992, Brown was head coach at Michigan Tech University in Houghton, Michigan. In 1991 he was runner-up in Coach of the Year voting within the Western Canadian Hockey Association.

Brown learned about coaching from one of the best while serving as an assistant coach and chief recruiter for Ron Mason at Michigan State University from 1987 to 1990. Brown names Mason and Dave King, the former Canadian Olympic and Calgary Flames NHL coach, as his major coaching influences in the game.

Brown was no less successful as a player. A native of Cornwall, Ontario, Brown played Major Junior for two seasons, helping Cornwall to a Memorial Cup title in 1980. He turned in a brilliant collegiate hockey career at Michigan State, serving as team captain during his senior year in 1983-84, when the squad reached the NCAA final four. For his play and leadership he received the Outstanding Senior Award.

He went on to play for Muskegon of the International Hockey League and Fredericton of the American Hockey League in 1985. The following year Brown was named team captain of the Canadian National Olympic team.

Vern Stenlund is one of the world's leading hockey instructors. He has played professional hockey and has coached the sport at all levels. Named head coach of the Windsor Spitfires in 1997, he is also a consultant to Huron Hockey School (HHS) and Director of Program Development for HHS.

A first-round choice of the London Knights of the Ontario Hockey League, Stenlund led the team in scoring with 119 points during the 1975-76 season. A second-round pick by the NHL's California Golden Seals in 1976, Stenlund eventually played for the Cleveland Barons of the NHL as well as for the Central Hockey League's Phoenix Roadrunners and Salt Lake City Eagles.

Stenlund began his coaching career directing the London Southwest Midgets of the Ontario Minor Hockey Association to a provincial championship in 1981-82. He has also coached at both the university and junior levels in Canada. He recently completed his fifth year as head coach of the league-champion Leamington Flyers of the Western Junior B League, where he has twice been voted Coach of the Year.

Stenlund is an assistant professor of education at the University of Windsor. He received an EdD from the University of Michigan in 1994. A former area scout for the NHL's Mighty Ducks of Anaheim, Stenlund is a consultant for Vitality Alliance, formerly the Praxis Group of Provo, Utah.

About Huron Hockey School

Huron has been the "first choice" in hockey schools since being created as a labor of love in 1970. The school was conceived and developed by Brian Gilmour, an All-American player at Boston University in 1967; Bill Mahoney, who would go on to coach the Minnesota North Stars in 1983; and Ron Mason, currently the most successful coach in college hockey history at Michigan State. All were young, analytical coaches who realized the need for a more scientific approach to teaching the fundamentals of their athletic passion. Their pioneering philosophy of "hockey by professional educators" changed the nature of hockey schools everywhere, which, until that time, had consisted primarily of summer camps visited by NHL stars. Sound teaching had not been the central focus.

Huron instructors were the first hockey school teachers to apply video analysis as a means of assessing the biomechanics of skating, first to develop a separate goalie program, first to offer specialized instruction for Junior "A" and NHL-caliber players, and first to establish satellite campus programs. The Huron curriculum—annually updated and expanded, and now including a roller hockey component—has been taught to more than 100,000 smiling, energized youngsters from across North America and around the world. Its success is symbolized by some 400 players and 40 coaches who have graduated to hockey's pinnacle, the National Hockey League. The list includes Marc Crawford, the coach of the 1996 Stanley Cup Champion Colorado Avalanche. He attended Huron as a teenager and remains associated with the school almost 20 years later.

Huron remains at the forefront as hockey's popularity explodes in the United States and worldwide, just like a slap shot off the stick of 1985 graduate Al MacInnis. From our new headquarters in Geneva, Illinois, the Huron team is embarking on an ambitious five-year corporate game plan designed to further the reach of the game's most innovative hockey group. The envisioned result will be a cutting-edge corporate entity involving arena building, management, and consulting computer software applications for hockey organizations; instructional videos and books, such as this one; and ownership and operation of junior-level hockey teams.

It's as true today as it was 27 years ago: Hockey continues to grow in popularity, and Huron continues to be the leader in hockey-related advances and innovations.

Paul O'Dacre
For Huron Hockey Group